Workbook

Our Faith and Worship

Companion to the Textbook
of Islamic 'Aqa'id and Arkan

Elementary Level • Volume 2

Hina Naseem

IQRA'
International Educational Foundation
Chicago

Part of a Comprehensive and Systematic Program of Islamic Studies

A Workbook for the Program of Islamic Studies Elementary Level

Our Faith and Worship: Volume 2

Chief Program Editors
Dr. Abidullah al-Ansari Ghazi
(Ph.D., History of Religion Harvard University)

Tasneema Ghazi
(Ph.D., Curriculum-Reading University of Minnesota)

Language Editing
Huseyn Abiva
University of Maryland

Reviewed by
Tasneema Ghazi

Design
Siddiqa Qazi

Second Printing November 2001
Third Printing June 2004
Printed at Stamford Press Pte Ltd, Singapore

IQRA' International Educational Foundation
7450 Skokie Blvd., Skokie, IL 60077
Website: www.iqra.com
Email: iqra@iqra.org

ISBN # 1-56316-065-X

IQRA's Note

We are pleased to introduce to you this study guide for the textbook *Our Faith and Worship Volume 2*. Study guides are an integral part of IQRA's Comprehensive Program of Islamic Education, along with their accompanying textbooks.

This Study Guide provides students with the opportunity to:

i. master the contents of the textbook
ii. develop better study skills
iii. internalize the knowledge of *Fiqh* and *'Aqidah* (*Sawm, Zakat, Hajj,* and *Jihad*)
iv. learn and develop critical thinking skills

We hope that teachers and parents will find the exercises and activities engaging and relevant. Through field testing, we have found that students have enjoyed working through this book. We hope and pray that every student will enjoy learning his/her *Din* through these books, *'Inshā' Allah.*

Please keep in touch and send us your comments and/or suggestions.

Chief Editors
IQRA' International
Educational Foundation

Workbook

Table of Contents

Lesson 1

THE ṢIYĀM: FASTING

1. To Become Better Muslims

A *Muttaqī* is a person who follows the straight path of Allāh ﷻ. What four good deeds can a *Muttaqī* do to show that he/she is following the straight path? (*Write one deed in each arrow.*)

a. b.

c. d.

2. Multiple Choice

Circle the letter of the word that makes the most sense in the sentence:

a. The purpose of fasting is to create _________ in our hearts.

a. *Hijrah*
b. *Ṣiyām*
c. *Taqwā*
d. *Muttaqūn*

b. Muslims must fast from __________ to __________.

a. *Aṣ-Ṣubh aṣ-Ṣādiq; Ishā*
b. *Fajr; Maghrib*
c. *Taqwā; Maghrib*
d. *Aṣ-Ṣubh aṣ-Ṣādiq; Maghrib*

3. Learning on Your Own - *The Islamic Calendar*

The Islamic calendar and the Gregorian calendar are different from each other. Look at an Islamic calendar and a Gregorian calendar, and tell two ways they are different from each other. (*Please see Appendix A*)

a. ____

____

____

____

b. ____

____

____

____

4. Writing Exercise

Allāh ﷻ says in the Qur'ān that "Fasting is prescribed to you as it was prescribed to those before you …" (2:183)

Research and write about the fasting prescribed and observed by one group of the People of the Book, Jews or Christians. Complete the following outline before writing your report:

THE PEOPLE

Name: ____________________

Book: ____________________

Prophet: ____________________

KIND OF FASTING

Farḍ ____________________

Nafl ____________________

Name(s) of fast(s) ____________________________________

How many days does the fast last? _______

During which months does it occur? ____________________

____

PRACTICES OF THE FAST(S)

Actions prohibited while fasting:

Actions encouraged while fasting:

Requirements for fasting:

Are there any special prayers for fasting?

Special food eaten to break the fast:

Celebrations after the fast:

5. Unscramble!!!!

The following words are things that Muslims must give up during *Ramadān*. As you are filling in the blanks, place the shaded letters in the box at the bottom to find out what Allāh ﷻ wants us to keep under control!

_ _ D   L _ N _ _ _ G _

F O O D

F _ G _ T _ _ _

C _ G _ R _ T _ _ S

_ U L _ Y _ _ G

_ R _ N _

U _ _ R _ T H _ _ L _ _ S _

What does Allāh ﷻ want us to keep under control?

_ _ _   _ _ _ _ _ _

6. The Control Issue

Allāh ﷻ is All-Knowing. He has given people the ability to control many things in their lives. In the following examples (given in the box), decide which ones are strictly under Allāh's ﷻ control and which ones Allāh ﷻ has let us control for ourselves, then write each example in one of the petals corresponding to who controls it.

- Having *Taqwā*.
- The Islamic Calendar is based on sightings of the moon.
- Keeping fast without breaking it.
- Fasting is prescribed during the month of *Ramaḍān*.
- Eating pork is *Ḥarām*.
- Eating pork.
- *Ṣawm* is a *Rukn* of Islam.
- We follow the right path of Islam.

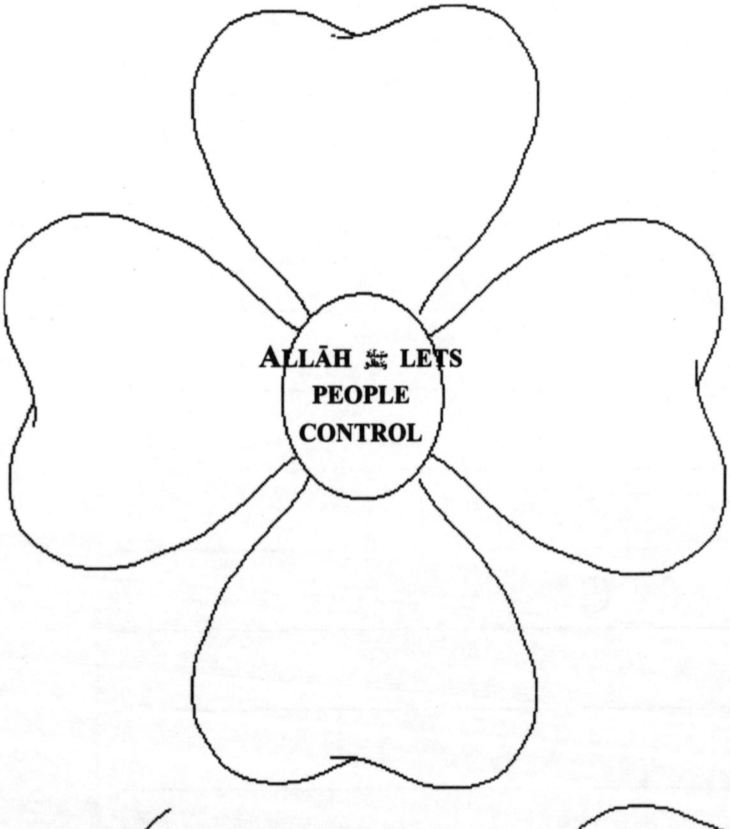

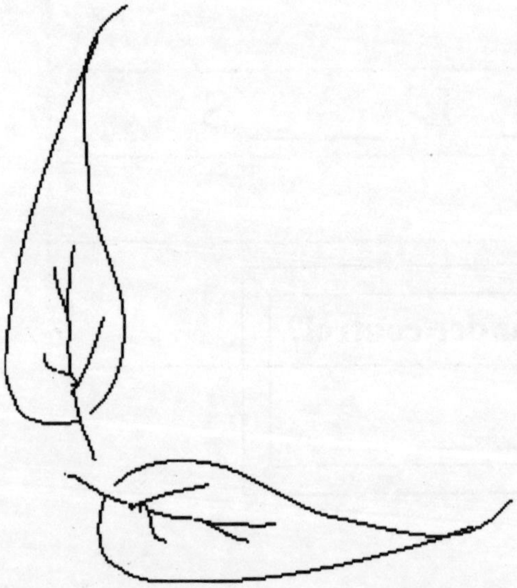

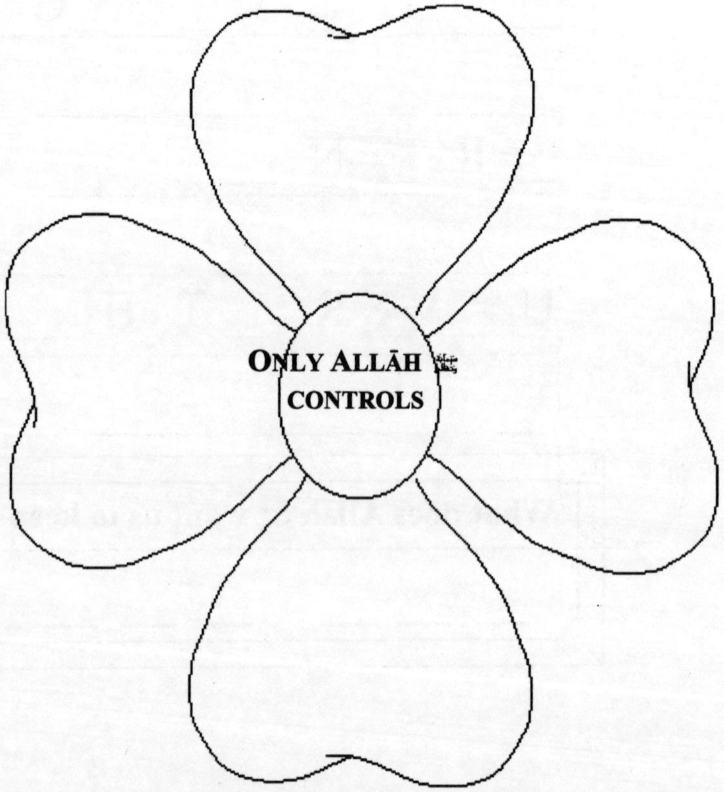

7. Qur'anic Study

Allāh ﷾ tells us in the Qur'ān:

وَكُلُوا۟ وَٱشْرَبُوا۟ حَتَّىٰ يَتَبَيَّنَ لَكُمُ ٱلْخَيْطُ ٱلْأَبْيَضُ مِنَ ٱلْخَيْطِ ٱلْأَسْوَدِ مِنَ ٱلْفَجْرِ ۖ

"*And eat and drink, until the white thread of dawn appear to you distinct from its black thread...*" (*Al-Baqarah*,2:187).

What does Allāh ﷾ mean when He refers to the 'white thread' and 'black thread'?

Lesson 2

THE MONTH OF THE QUR'ĀN

1. The Blessed Month

Give three reasons why *Ramaḍān* is such a blessed month.

a. ____________________

b. ____________________

c. ____________________

2. Let's Celebrate Ramadan !!

Ramaḍān is a very special month for Muslims. Put an "X" through the balloons containing things we cannot do to celebrate during *Ramaḍān*.

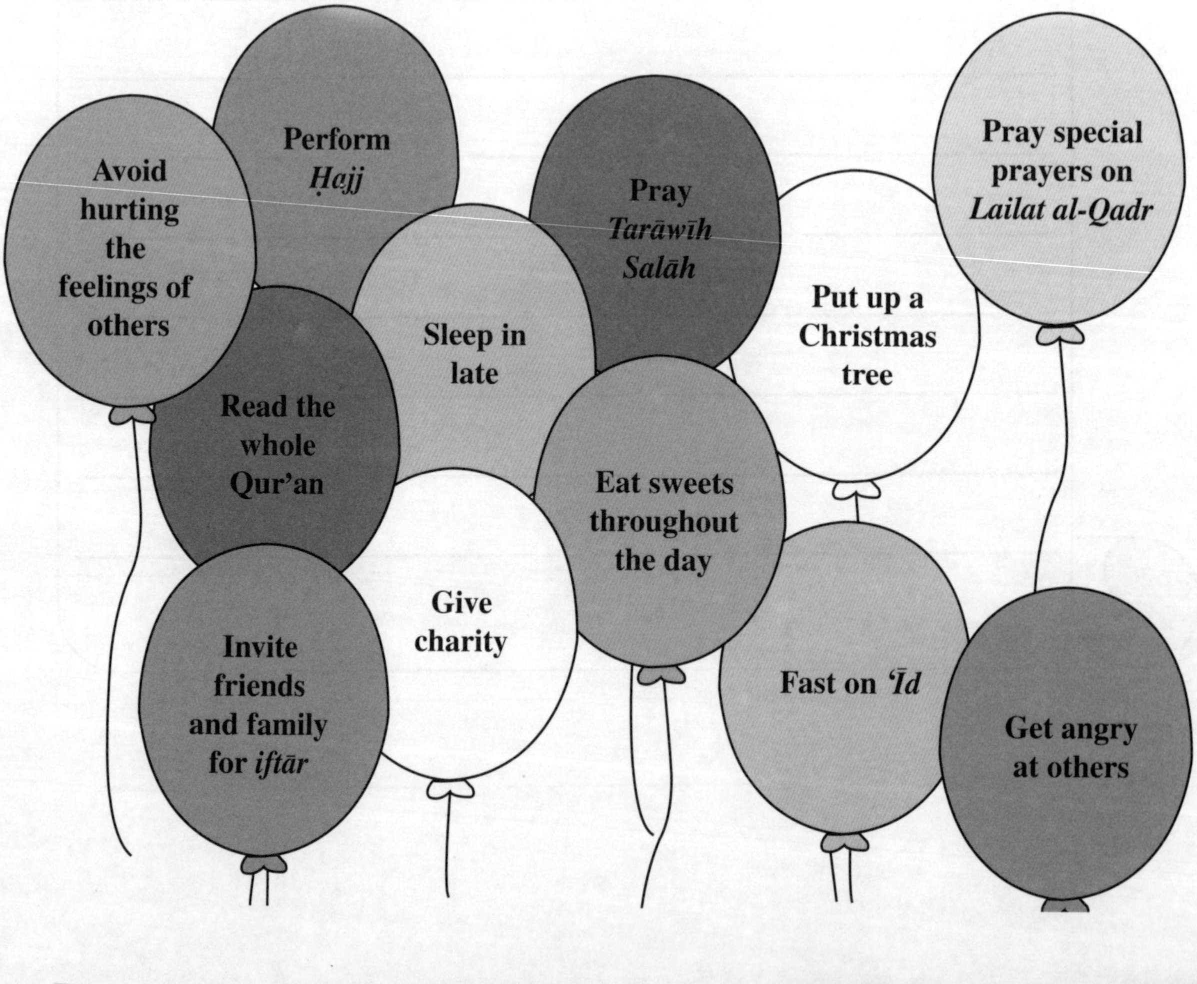

3. Think About It!!

What does Allāh ﷻ mean when He says that "The Night of Power is better than a thousand months"? (*Al-Qadr, 97:3*)

لَيْلَةُ ٱلْقَدْرِ خَيْرٌ مِّنْ أَلْفِ شَهْرٍ ﴿٣﴾

____

____

____

____

____

4. Vocabulary

Use the following words in a complete sentence:

a. *Tarāwīḥ*: ____

____

b. *Ḥāfiz*: ____

____

c. *Qāri'*: ____

____

d. *Iftār*: ____

____

5. To Become Better Muslims

Write or draw your plans for two charitable activities you would like to do during the next *Ramaḍān*.

1.

2.

6. Learning on Your Own - *Using the Qur'an as a Tool to Gain Knowledge*

'Umar has certain questions about Islam. Help him think of the key word for each example so 'Umar can look it up in the index of the Qur'ān and find the answer to his questions. (*Use Abdullah Yusuf Ali's translation.*)

a. What book was revealed in the month of *Ramaḍān*? (2:185) ____________________

b. Who can receive *Zakāh* money? (2:177) ____________________

c. How was Iblīs, a *jinn*, created? (7:12) ____________________

d. Toward what direction do we face while praying? (2:144-145) ____________________

e. Is the Night of Power better than other nights? (97:1-3) ____________________

7. Qur'anic Study

Read *'āyah* 185 of *Surah Al-Baqarah* (given below) and write, in your own words, how Allāh سبحانه وتعالى does not want to put us through difficulty. (*Space for writing is given on the following page.*)

شَهْرُ رَمَضَانَ ٱلَّذِىٓ أُنزِلَ فِيهِ
ٱلْقُرْءَانُ هُدًى لِّلنَّاسِ وَبَيِّنَـٰتٍ مِّنَ ٱلْهُدَىٰ وَٱلْفُرْقَانِ ۚ فَمَن شَهِدَ مِنكُمُ
ٱلشَّهْرَ فَلْيَصُمْهُ ۖ وَمَن كَانَ مَرِيضًا أَوْ عَلَىٰ سَفَرٍ فَعِدَّةٌ مِّنْ أَيَّامٍ أُخَرَ ۗ
يُرِيدُ ٱللَّهُ بِكُمُ ٱلْيُسْرَ وَلَا يُرِيدُ بِكُمُ ٱلْعُسْرَ وَلِتُكْمِلُوا۟ ٱلْعِدَّةَ وَلِتُكَبِّرُوا۟
ٱللَّهَ عَلَىٰ مَا هَدَىٰكُمْ وَلَعَلَّكُمْ تَشْكُرُونَ ﴿١٨٥﴾

The month of Ramadân in which was revealed the Qur'ân, a guidance for mankind and clear proofs for the guidance and the criterion (between right and wrong). So whoever of you sights (the crescent on the first night of) the month (of Ramadân i.e. is present at his home), he must observe Saum (fasts) that month, and whoever is ill or on a journey, the same number [of days which one did not observe Saum (fasts) must be made up] from other days. Allâh intends for you ease, and He does not want to make things difficult for you. (He wants that you) must complete the same number (of days), and that you must magnify Allâh [i.e. to say Takbîr (Allâhu-Akbar; Allâh is the Most Great) on seeing the crescent of the months of Ramadân and Shawwâl] for having guided you so that you may be grateful to Him.
(*Al-Baqarah*, 2:185)

Lesson 3

THE FASTING: AN OBLIGATION

1. Fundamentals of Fasting

As we have read in our textbook, there are two kinds of fasting. In the graphic organizer below, list the two types of fasts, then write down the characteristic of each type of fast underneath.

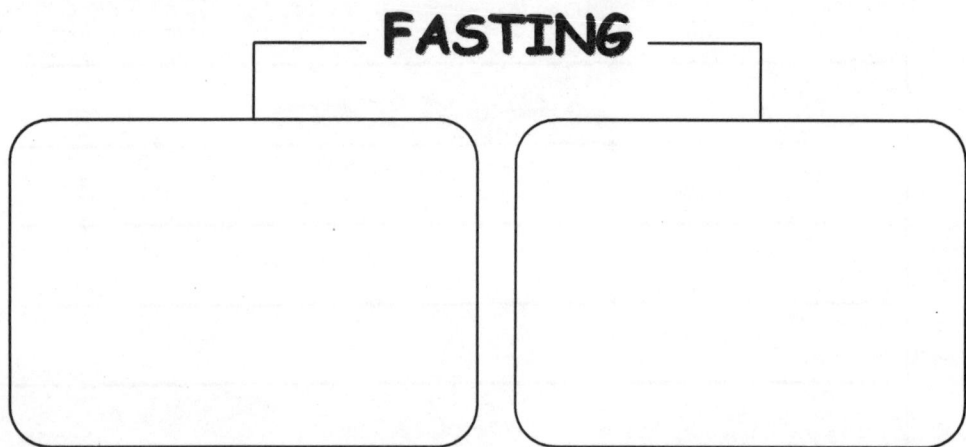

FASTING

2. Think About It!!

Write in your own words the *niyyah* of fasting.

Why is it important to make *niyyah* before we fast?

3. Did I Forget My Fast?

Which of the following actions will break the fast? If the action results in breaking the fast, circle "B"; if the action leaves the fast unbroken, circle "U".

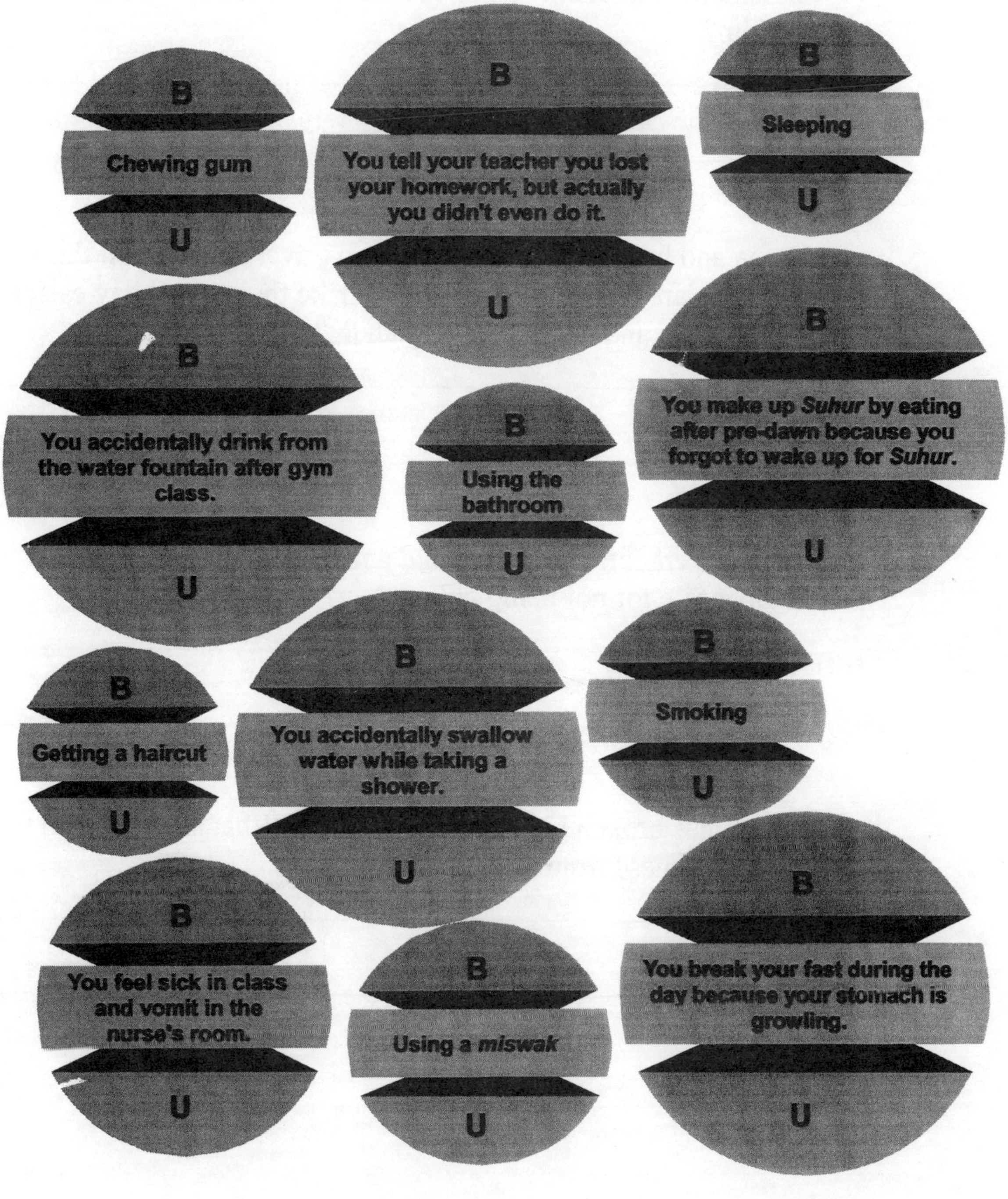

B
Chewing gum
U
B
You tell your teacher you lost your homework, but actually you didn't even do it.
U
B
Sleeping
U
B
You accidentally drink from the water fountain after gym class.
U
B
Using the bathroom
U
B
You make up *Suhur* by eating after pre-dawn because you forgot to wake up for *Suhur*.
U
B
Getting a haircut
U
B
You accidentally swallow water while taking a shower.
U
B
Smoking
U
B
You feel sick in class and vomit in the nurse's room.
U
B
Using a *miswak*
U
B
You break your fast during the day because your stomach is growling.
U

4. What Do I Do?

The children mentioned below have run into some problems about fasting. Can you help them answer their questions of what to do?

a. Idris is fasting. During lunchtime at school he watches his classmates eat lunch. What can Idris do to make his fast easier for him?

____

____

b. Huma and her family are planning to travel to Egypt on the 10th of Ramadān. What can they do to make their travel day easier in Ramadān and not disobey Allāh ﷻ?

____

____

c. Rashid's grandfather is very old and sick. What can he do to compensate for not being able to fast?

____

____

d. Hamid has broken his fast intentionally. What should he do to get forgiveness from Allāh ﷻ?

____

____

5. Flowchart

Flowcharts are a way to show steps and decisions that are made to complete a task. There are certain symbols used in flowcharts that allow you to organize how you will complete your task. Using the symbols and example given below, fill in the blank steps in the flowchart:

Symbols

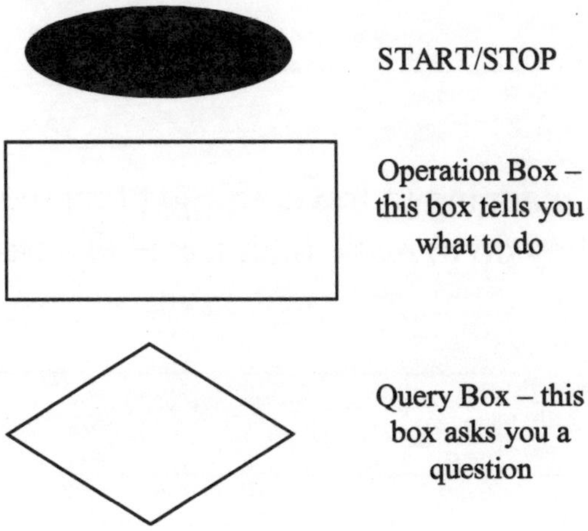

Example

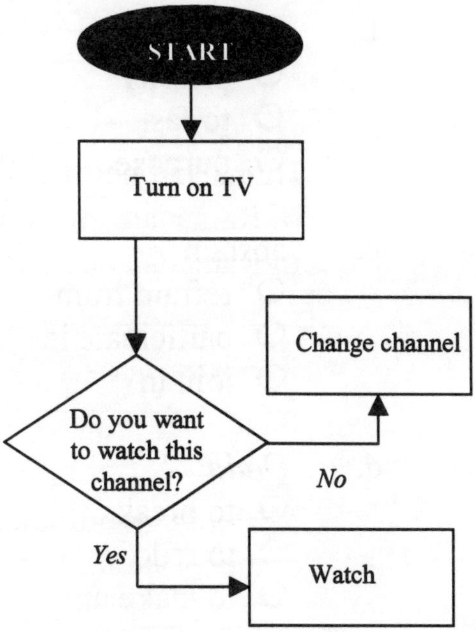

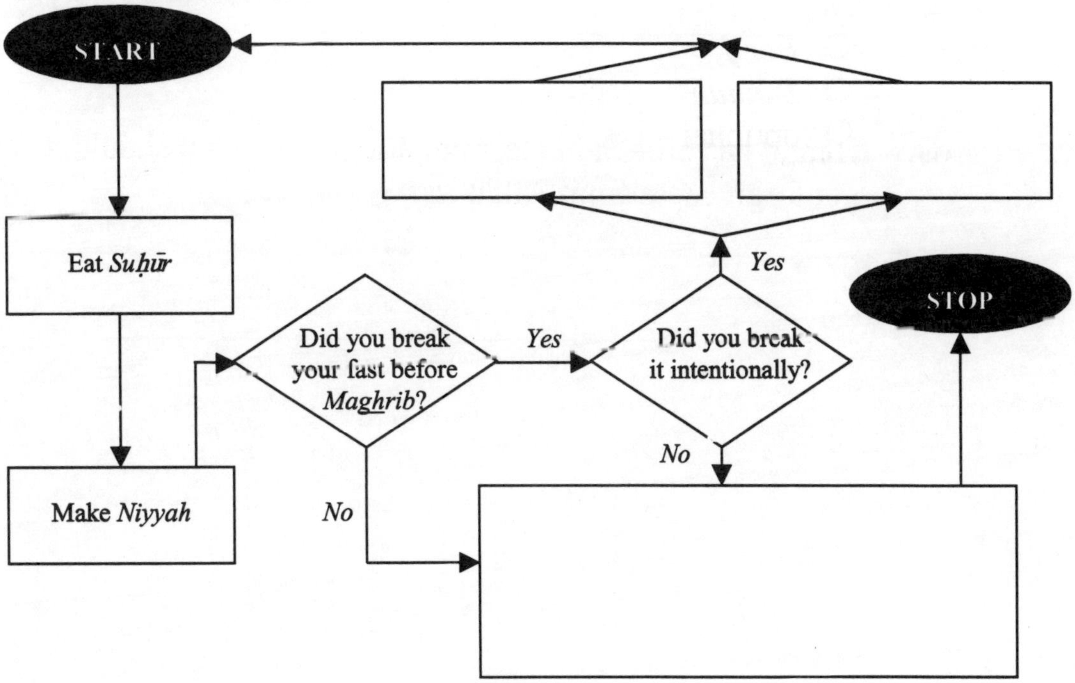

6. Vocabulary

Use your textbook or a dictionary to help you choose the word/phrase that best describes the vocabulary word:

a. genuine
- ❍ artifical
- ❍ real
- ❍ imaginary

b. intention
- ❍ priority
- ❍ to fast
- ❍ purpose

c. abstain
- ❍ refrain from
- ❍ participate in
- ❍ join in

d. *Qadā*
- ❍ to break
- ❍ to redo
- ❍ to make up

e. *Nafl*
- ❍ *Farḍ*
- ❍ *Sunnah*
- ❍ optional

7. Qur'anic Study

In *'āyah* 2:184, given below, Allāh سبحانه وتعالى mentions some of the things we can do to make up for any days missed fasting due to some hardship. What do we have to do is we miss these days on purpose or *kaffarah*?

فَمَن كَانَ مِنكُم مَّرِيضًا أَوْ عَلَىٰ سَفَرٍ فَعِدَّةٌ مِّنْ أَيَّامٍ أُخَرَ

But if any of you is sick or on a trip, the days missed should be made up from later days.
(*Al-Baqarah*, 2:184)

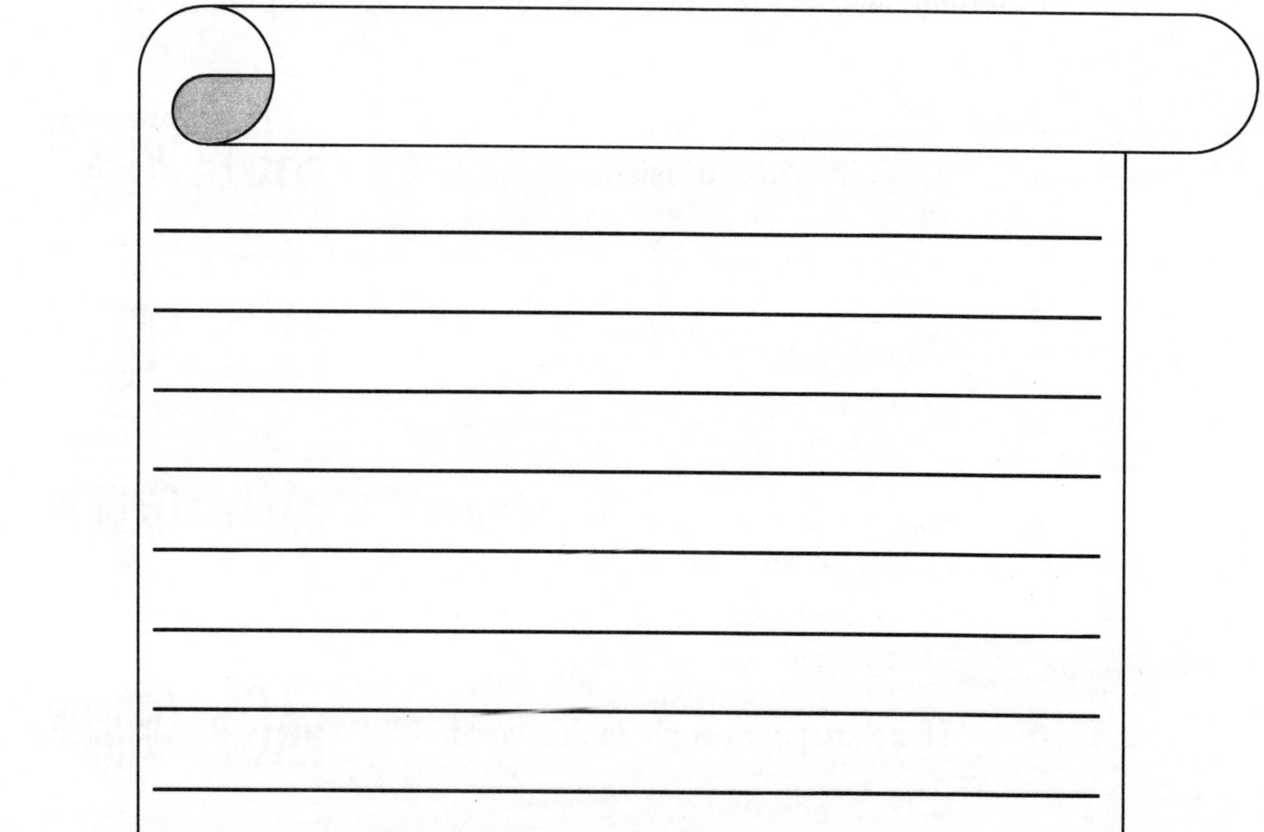

Lesson 4

THE ZAKĀH

1. Fact or Opinion?

A **fact** is something that is true or said to be true. For example, "his car is red," or "Egypt is a country." An **opinion** is a statement describing a personal belief that isn't necessarily true. For example, "the stars are pretty," or "cookies are everybody's favorite food."

Determine whether the following statements are fact or opinion:

a. *Zakāh* is a *Rukn* of Islam — FACT OPINION

b. I like giving *Zakāh* — FACT OPINION

c. *Zakāh* is mentioned alongside *Salāh* in the Qur'ān — FACT OPINION

d. There are poor people in the world. — FACT OPINION

e. Sharing is fun!!! — FACT OPINION

2. Parts of Speech

A **noun** is a person, place or thing. For example, Malaysia, flower and father are all nouns. An adjective is a word that describes a noun. For example, *pretty*, *juicy*, *furry*, and *helpful* are all adjectives.

a. Match the correct adjective with the noun.

Qur'ān	**Pure**
Duty	**Clean**
Clothes	**Sincere**
'Ibādāt	**Holy**
Wealth	**Islamic**

b. Select the appropriate adjective that accurately describes each of the following nouns, and write it in the space provided.
ADJECTIVES: **merciful, *farḍ*, true, Muslim, *ḥalāl*, Islamic**

______________ *Ummah'* ______________ responsibility

______________ *Ṣalāh* ______________ believer

______________ blessings ______________ Allāh سُبْحَانَهُ وَتَعَالَى

3. Finish the Thought

When I am older and will give *Zakāh*, doing this action will make me feel.....

4. Something on Family (*'Ummah*)

As we read in the following hadith of Rasūlullāh ﷺ, we are told that Muslims must love each other and care for each other as if we are all one body. List below some of the ways we can show love and care to our Muslim brothers and sisters around the world.

و عن النَّعْمَان بَشِير رضي الله عنهما قال: قال رسول الله صلى الله
عليه و سلم: «مَثَلُ الْمُؤْمِنِينَ فِي تَوَادِّهِمْ وَ تَرَاحُمِهِمْ وَ تَعَاطُفِهِمْ، مَثَلُ
الْجَسَدِ إِذَا اشْتَكَى مِنْهُ عُضْوٌ تَدَاعَى لَهُ سَائِرُ الْجَسَدِ بِالسَّهَرِ وَ
الْحُمَّى» متفقٌ عليه.

Allah's Apostle ﷺ said: "You see the believers as regards their being merciful among themselves and showing love among themselves and being kind, resembling one body, so that, if any part of the body is not well then the whole body shares the sleeplessness (insomnia) amd fever with it." (Sahih al-Bukhari, narrated by An-Numan Bashir)

5. Vocabulary

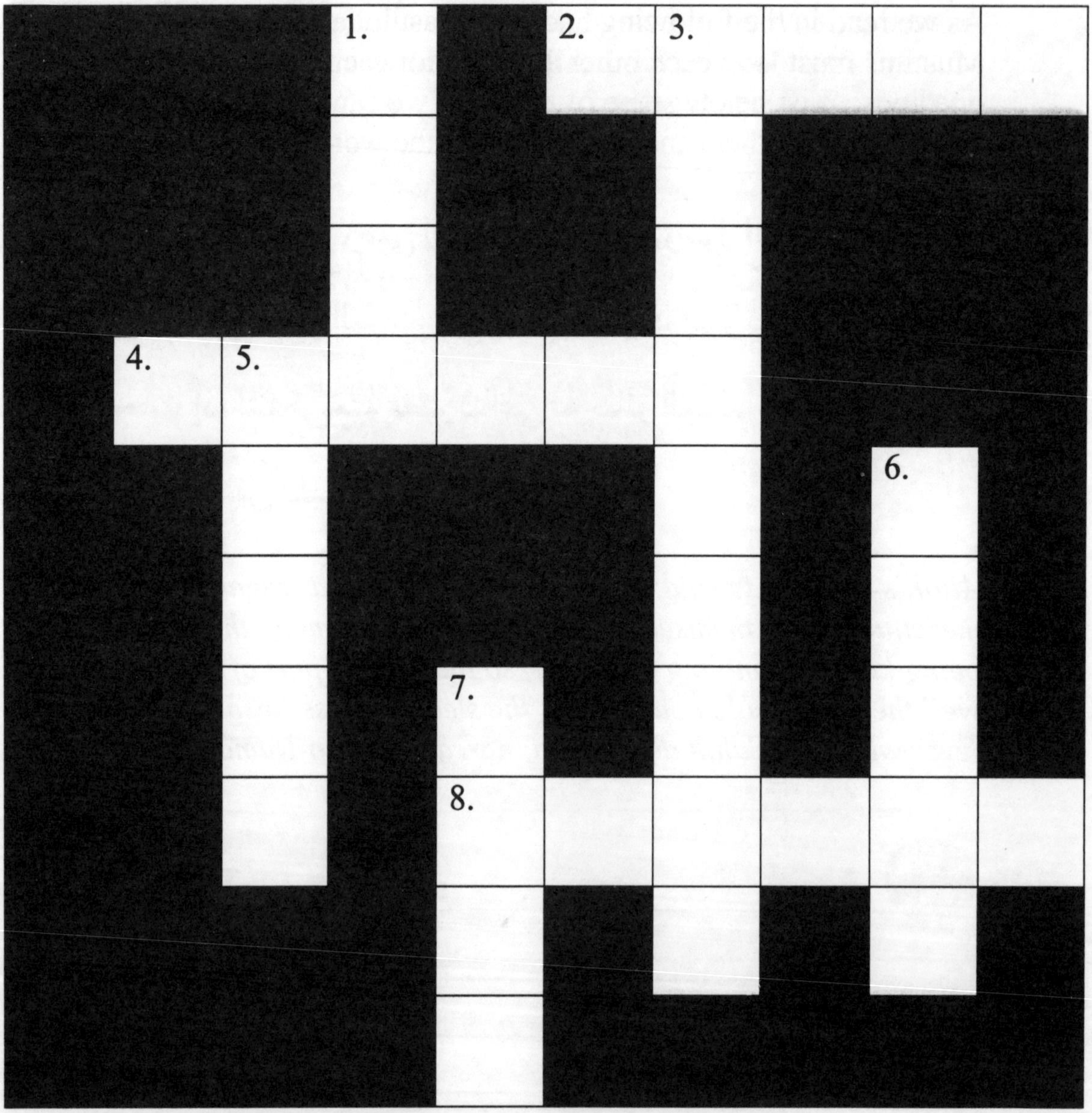

DOWN

1. Muslims give *Zakāh* to the ____.
3. Holy Book.
5. Family in Islam.
6. Arabic word meaning "make something purified"
7. Everything we have is a ____ from Allāh سبحانه وتعالى

ACROSS

2. We have to ____ our wealth with the poor and needy.
4. By giving *Zakāh*, we ____ our wealth.
8. *Zakāh* is an act of ____.

6. Qur'anic Study

Read the *'āyah* given below. In reality, who receives our gifts of charity? Why do you think Allāh سبحانه وتعالى always mentions charity and forgiveness of sins together?

أَلَمْ يَعْلَمُوٓا۟ أَنَّ ٱللَّهَ هُوَ يَقْبَلُ ٱلتَّوْبَةَ عَنْ عِبَادِهِۦ وَيَأْخُذُ

ٱلصَّدَقَٰتِ وَأَنَّ ٱللَّهَ هُوَ ٱلتَّوَّابُ ٱلرَّحِيمُ ﴿١٠٤﴾

Do they not know that Allah does accept repentance from His worshippers and receives their gifts of charity and that Allāh is truly He, the Acceptor of Repentence, the Most Merciful.
(*At-Taubah*, 9:104)

Lesson 5

THE NISĀB FOR THE ZAKĀH

1. Check it Off!

Farḍ is an activity which Allāh ﷻ requires us to do. In the following list, select which activities are *Farḍ* for every adult Muslim.

❑ *Ḥajj*

❑ *Zakāh*

❑ Greeting Muslims with *Assalāmu alai-kum*

❑ *Ṣalāh*

❑ *Ṣaum*

❑ Reading and Writing

2. Fundamentals of Zakah

Name four items on which we have to pay *Zakāh*.

3. Think About It!

Laila has $10,000 in the bank. She has put $7,500 in her checking account to use for school, rent, groceries, etc. and put the rest in her savings. How much will her *Zakāh* payment be for that year? (**Remember – you pay Zakāh on savings!!*)

4. Differences and Similarities

How are *Ṣadaqah* and *Zakāh* different? How are they alike? List one in each of the fruits.

DIFFERENCES **SIMILARITIES**

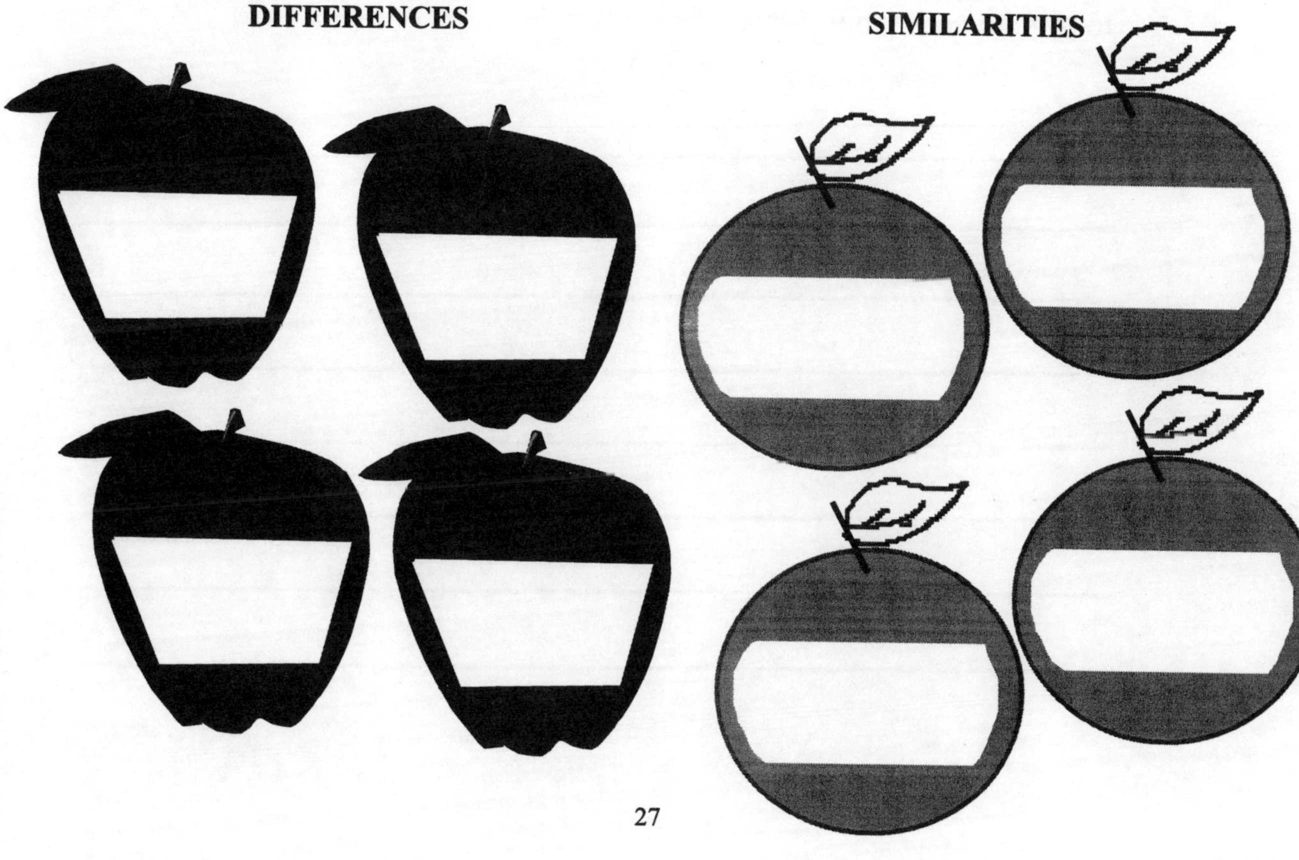

5. What Do I Do?

Mustafa has been working for two years after finishing his studies. He borrowed $1,000 from his brother while he was in college, to help pay for school expenses. He has been able to save up the amount of *Nisab*. Is he required to pay *Zakah*? Why or why not?

6. Creative Writing

In a brief paragraph, write about a *Hadaya* (gift) which you would like to give to someone special.

7. Vocabulary

Read Lesson 5, then write the antonyms, or words that have the opposite meanings, of the following words:

maximum → ______________________

unkind → ______________________

discourage → ______________________

punishment → ______________________

ḥarām → ______________________

before → ______________________

generous → ______________________

spend → ______________________

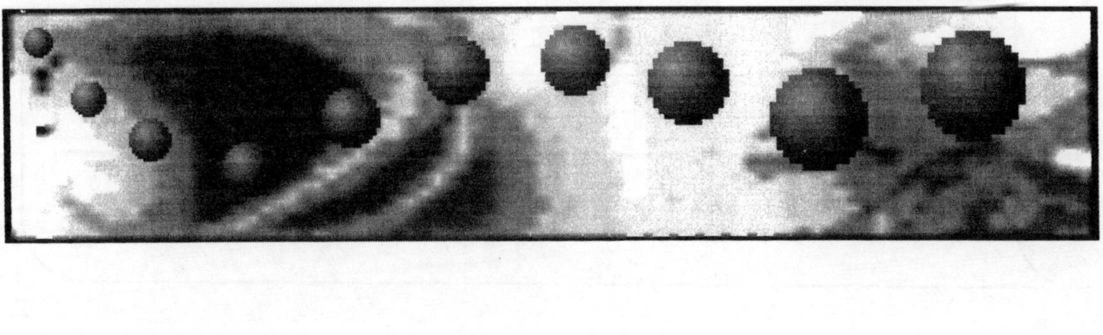

8. Qur'anic Study

Read the following *'āyah*. What is the credit that Allāh سبحانه وتعالى will donate if we give *Qarḍ Ḥasanah* (a beautiful loan)?

إِن تُقْرِضُوا۟ ٱللَّهَ قَرْضًا حَسَنًا يُضَٰعِفْهُ لَكُمْ وَيَغْفِرْ قَرْضًا
حَسَنًا يُضَٰعِفْهُ لَكُمْ وَيَغْفِرْ لَكُمْ ۚ وَٱللَّهُ شَكُورٌ حَلِيمٌ ﴿١٧﴾

If you loan to Allah a beautiful loan, He will double it for you and He will give you forgiveness, for Allah is the Most Appreciative and Tolerant.
(*At-Taghābūn*, 64:17)

Lesson 6

THE PAYMENT OF ZAKĀH

1. Where Does Our Money Go?

In the United States, we can use our tax money for donations to not-for-profit organizations. Allāh ﷻ asks us to use our *Zakāh* money to help the needy and the poor.

In the list below, decide whether the following people or organizations can receive United States government (federal) tax money, *Zakāh*, or both. Check the appropriate box to indicate your answer.

	U.S. Tax Money	Zakāt Tax Money	Both
1. Orphanages for poor Muslim orphans	☐	○	☐
2. Soup Kitchen for the homeless	☐	○	☐
3. To win the hearts of non-Muslims for the Muslim community	☐	○	☐
4. Officials who work for the collection of *Zakāh*	☐	○	☐
5. To build a *Masjid*	☐	○	☐
6. To build a mansion for the President	☐	○	☐
7. To build public schools	☐	○	☐

2. *Sadaqah* or *Zakat*

Put a "Z" in the right scale next to the sentences that describe examples of to whom you, as an individual, may pay *Zakah*. Then put an "S" in the left scale next to those examples that are *Ṣadaqah*.

Your neighborhood asks for donations for a neighborhood watch

A Muslim in your community doesn't have enough money to pay off a debt.

A young Muslim man cannot go to college because his family's income does not cover school tuition.

A Muslim overseas has lost his home and family.

Your sister needs money so she can perform the *Ḥajj*.

A Muslim convert is struggling to establish herself in the Muslim community.

A national agency asks you to donate towards the cause of cancer research.

3. Think about It!!

Zakāh money should be used to free a slave from the bondage of slavery. Read the story of freedom of the great *Ṣaḥābi* and *muadhdhin* of *Rasūlullāh* ﷺ, Bilāl ibn Rabāḥ ؓ from the bondage of slavery through Abu Bakr's ؓ great donation, found in The Lives of Al-Khulafā' Ar-Rāshidūn (Iqra', 1998). Retell the story in your own words below. Then tell the story to your brothers, sisters and friends.

4. Multiple Choice

Circle the correct answer for each of the following:

a. *Zakah* is _____.

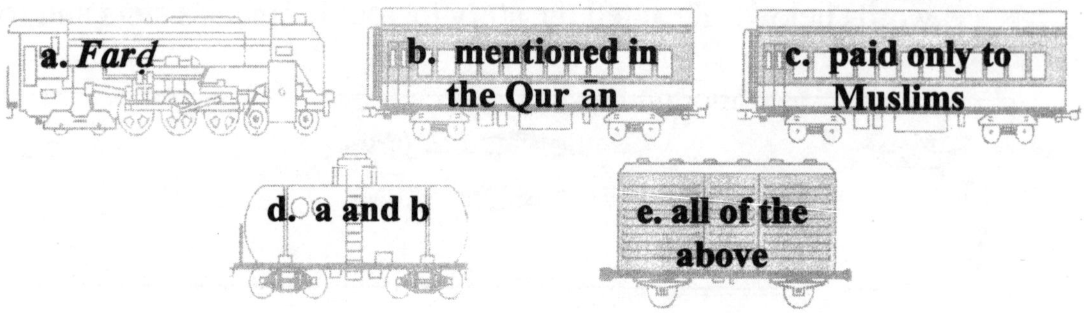

b. *Zakah* is obligatory only on _____.

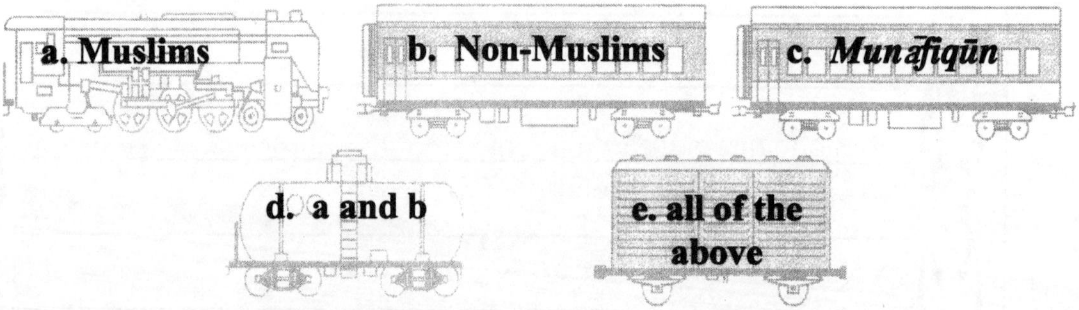

c. *Zakah* money can be given to _____.

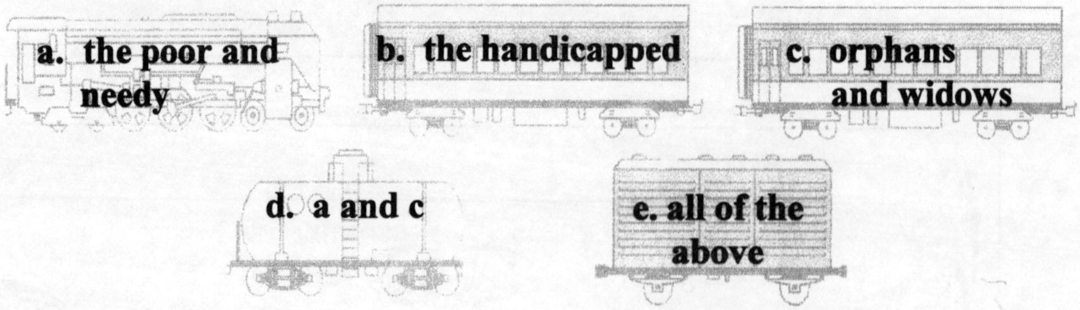

5. Fill in the Blanks

Read page 12 of the textbook and fill in the following blanks:

a. __________ is a special favor of Allāh ﷻ to Muslims.

b. Even though he/she may possess *Nisāb*, an __________ or a __________ do not need to pay *Zakāh*.

c. __________ who work to collect *Zakāh* can get their salary from the *Zakāh* funds.

6. Vocabulary

For each statement given, complete the phrase to most closely exemplify the same relationship.

1. Homelessness is to the poor, as property is to the _____.
   a. rich b. wayfarer c. needy

2. Independence is to freedom, as bondage is to _____.
   a. poverty b. slavery c. charity

3. Pleased is to displeased, as recommended is to _____.
   a. suggested b. rejected c. accepted

7. Qur'anic Study

Generosity in charity is so important in Islam that it is one of the five major pillars of Islam, which every Muslim must follow. According to the *'āyah* given below, is it important to tell people when you give charity? Why or why not? Why does Allāh ﷻ say it is better to give in secret?

إِن تُبْدُوا۟ ٱلصَّدَقَٰتِ فَنِعِمَّا هِىَ ۖ وَإِن تُخْفُوهَا وَتُؤْتُوهَا ٱلْفُقَرَآءَ فَهُوَ
خَيْرٌ لَّكُمْ ۚ وَيُكَفِّرُ عَنكُم مِّن سَيِّـَٔاتِكُمْ ۗ وَٱللَّهُ بِمَا تَعْمَلُونَ خَبِيرٌ ﴿٢٧١﴾

If you announce your charities it is fine, but if you hide them and make them reach those in need that is best for you. It will remove from you some of your bad deed, and Allah knows well whatever you do.
(*Al-Baqarah*, 2:271)

Lesson 7

THOSE WHO CANNOT RECEIVE ZAKĀH

1. Learning on Your Own – Where *Zakah* Money Goes

Think and write below the institutions in your community who can collect *Zakāh*. Interview the leaders of these institutions to find out how they distribute the money collected. Report to your class on your findings.

ORGANIZATION NAME	HOW FUNDS ARE DISTRIBUTED
LEADER'S NAME	

ORGANIZATION NAME	HOW FUNDS ARE DISTRIBUTED
LEADER'S NAME	

ORGANIZATION NAME	HOW FUNDS ARE DISTRIBUTED
LEADER'S NAME	

2. Think about It!!

Why do you think a Muslim can't give *Zakāh* to close family members?

3. True/False

Mark each statement as true or false. If the statement is false, cross out what is false and fill in the appropriate information to make the statement true.

round

Example: *False* The earth is ~~flat~~.

_____ Any member from the family of Rasūlullāh (ﷺ) (*Bait al-Māl*) cannot receive *Zakāh*.

_____ People who have wealth must pay *Zakāh* according to *Nisāb*, not receive it.

_____ *Zakāh* is the maximum amount a Muslim is required to pay if he/she has *Nisāb*.

_____ *Qarḍ Ḥasanah* is a no-interest loan.

4. Word Changers

You will make a list of words by changing letters. You can only change one letter (*although you can add more letters*).

EXAMPLE: P O S T office

L O S T and found

Not first, but L A S T

A L I S T of names

Muslims must give money to the ____ ____ ____ ____ .

Asad will ____ ____ ____ ____ the water.

There are five, not ____ ____ ____ ____ pillars of Islam.

The Qur'ān is our ____ ____ ____ ____ ____ ____ of Allāh's سبحانه وتعالى commands.

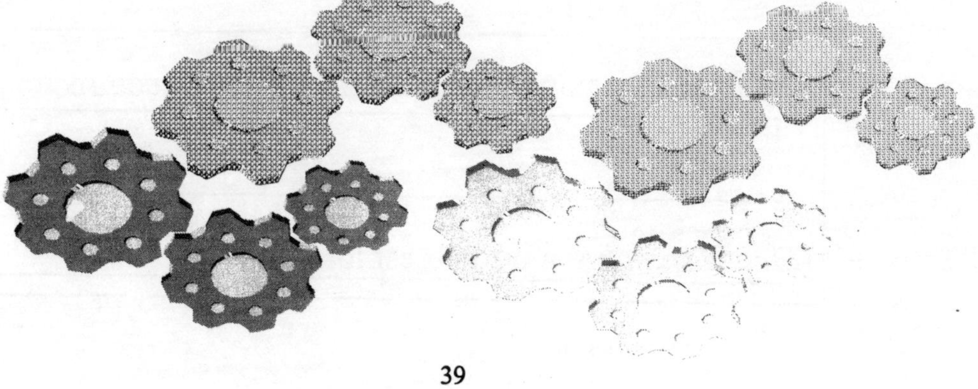

5. Reason through It!!

Solve the following problems:

a. All Muslims who have *Nisāb* must pay *Zakāh*. Muslims who pay *Zakāh* cannot receive *Zakāh*. Who then receives *Zakāh*? (*be very specific*)

b. Immediate family members cannot receive *Zakāh*. Ahmad and Sarah are Amjad's parents. Can Ahmad and Sarah receive *Zakāh* from Amjad?

6. Vocabulary

Select the word that most closely gives the meaning of the word given. Put an "X" through the two clouds that do <u>not</u> give the meaning.

7. Qur'anic Study

Many people only give charity when they have lots of money to spare. But what does Allāh سبحانه وتعالى say about those who spend even when they have some financial hardship? Also, look up in *hadīth* books some ways we can give charity even if we don't have money to spare. List these. (*see Appendix C*)

ٱلَّذِينَ يُنفِقُونَ فِى ٱلسَّرَّآءِ وَٱلضَّرَّآءِ وَٱلۡكَـٰظِمِينَ
ٱلۡغَيۡظَ وَٱلۡعَافِينَ عَنِ ٱلنَّاسِۗ وَٱللَّهُ يُحِبُّ ٱلۡمُحۡسِنِينَ ﴿١٣٤﴾

Those who give charity whether in good or bad times, who hold their anger and forgive people, Allah loves those who do good.
(*Al-'Imrān*, 3:134)

Lesson 8

ḤAJJ: THE PILGRIMAGE TO MAKKAH

---

1. A Little Bit of History

Who were the two prophets who built and rebuilt the *Ka'bah*?

a.____________________ b.____________________

2. Fill in the Blanks

The name for *Bait Allāh* in English is ____________________,
and in the center of this masjid is the Sacred M________________
around which we perform the ____________________.

3. Think about It!!

Imagine that you lived in Makkah during the time before Rasūlullāh's ﷺ birth. What might the *Ka'bah* have been like? Do you think it was surrounded by the *masjid* that is there now?

I don't think so because people on that
time din't really know that the kaba
is masjid, and

4. Analogies

An **analogy** is a relation between two pairs of words or phrases. The words in each pair must be related to each other in the same way.

EXAMPLE: Father is to man, as mother is to woman.

Solve the following analogies:

a. *Ṣaum* is to *Ramadān*, as *Ḥajj* is to ~~prey~~________.

b. Christianity is to Christian, as Islam is to Muslim________.

c. Yūsuf ﵇ is to Yaqūb ﵇, as Ismā'īl ﵇ is to Ibrahim________ ﵇.

d. *Rukū'* is to *Salāh*, as *Tawāf* is to walking kaba________.

e. House is to live, as masjid is to prey________.

5. Opposites

Look at the following words and think what they mean. Then, write down the word that best describes its opposite.

Shirk → ← ________

Barren → ← ________

'Imān → ← ________

6. Vocabulary

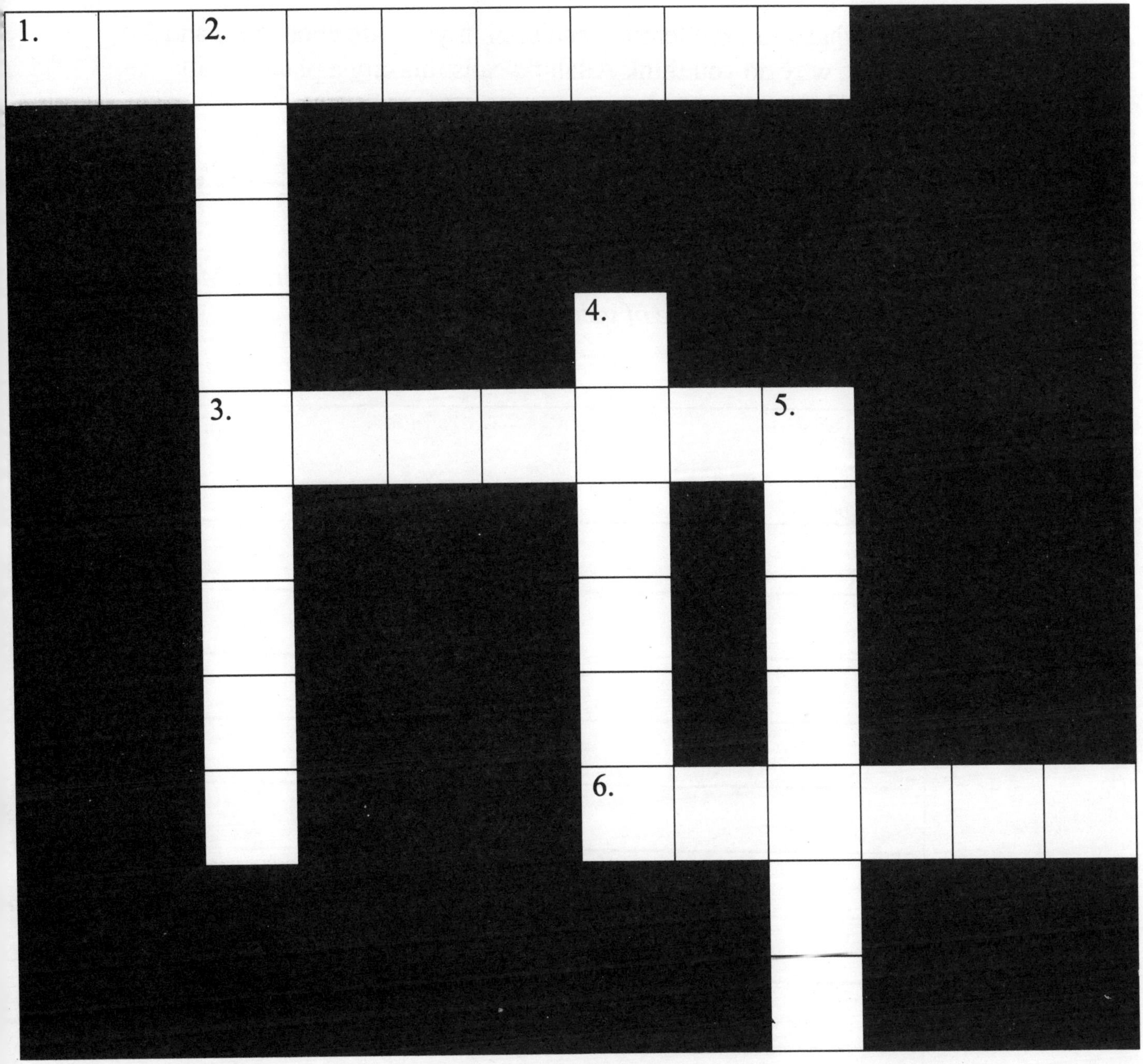

DOWN

2. To give up something precious in the way of Allāh سبحانه وتعالى
4. The Wisdom
5. Filled with anger

ACROSS

1. Descendents (children and their children) of a person
3. A tendency
6. Not Hell, but _____.

7. Qur'anic Study

Using what you have learned and seen in your life about *Ḥajj* and Makkah, why do you think Allāh ﷻ calls this city a place for all mankind?

إِنَّ أَوَّلَ بَيْتٍ وُضِعَ لِلنَّاسِ لَلَّذِى بِبَكَّةَ مُبَارَكًا وَهُدًى لِّلْعَٰلَمِينَ ﴿٩٦﴾

Indeed it is the first House built for all humans in the city of Makkah which is a blessed place of guidance for mankind.
(*Al-'Imrān*, 3:96)

Lesson 9

THE STORY OF MAKKAH

1. Who Am I???

Use the clues provided to find out who the mystery person is. Write the name of the person in the space provided.

a.
- I was the powerful king of Harrān.
- Some people worshipped me.
- I put Ibrāhim عليه السلام into the fire

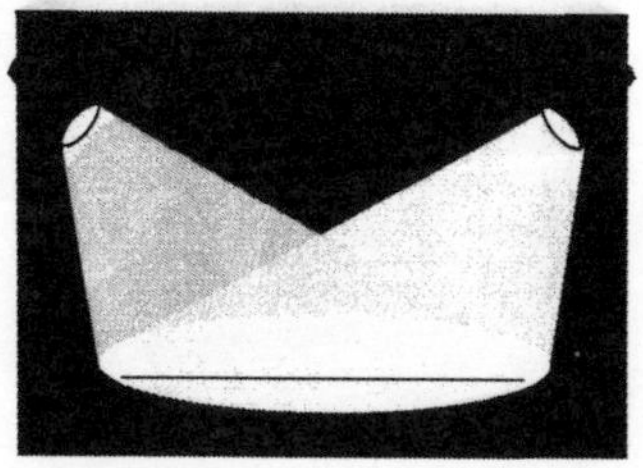

WHO AM I???

b.
- I lived in the city of Harrān.
- I was an idolmaker
- My son became a prophet of Allāh سبحانه وتعالى

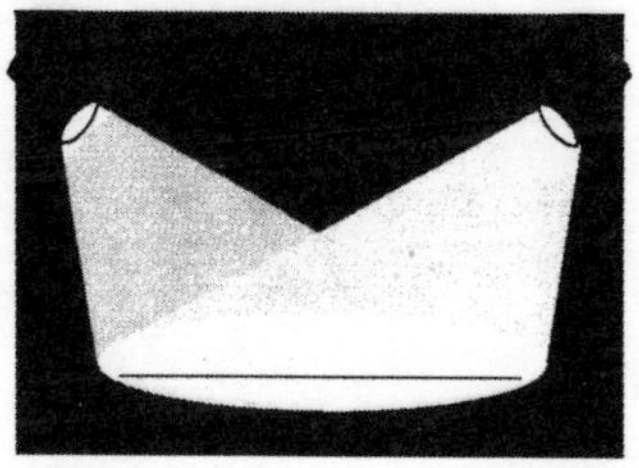

WHO AM I???

c.
- I settled in a land called Bakkah.
- I married Ibrāhim عليه السلام
- My son's name is Ismā'īl عليه السلام.

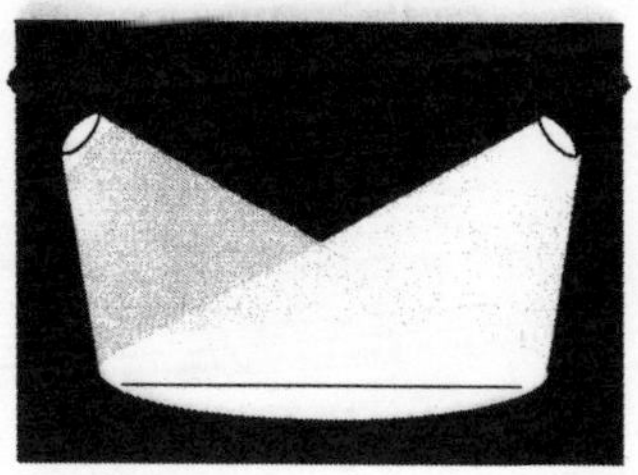

WHO AM I???

2. Unscramble

Unscramble the words to form meaningful, complete sentences.

a. blessed *Ḥikmah* Ibrāhīm ﷵ with was

____

b. Ibrāhīm ﷵ wīves Sarah had and named two Hājar

____

c. told Hājar Ibrāhīm ﷵ take Allāh ﷻ to to valley Ismā'īl ﷵ a Bakkah barren and called

____

____

d. name and *Ka'bah* located it another for is *Bait Allāh* is the the city is in Makkah of

____

____

e. Bakkah because in Hājar Allāh ﷻ stayed it commanded

____

____

3. Think about It!!

How do you think Ibrāhīm ﷷ felt about having to leave his family alone in the desert?

4. Vocabulary

Read each group of words and cross out the word in each group that does <u>not</u> belong with the other words.

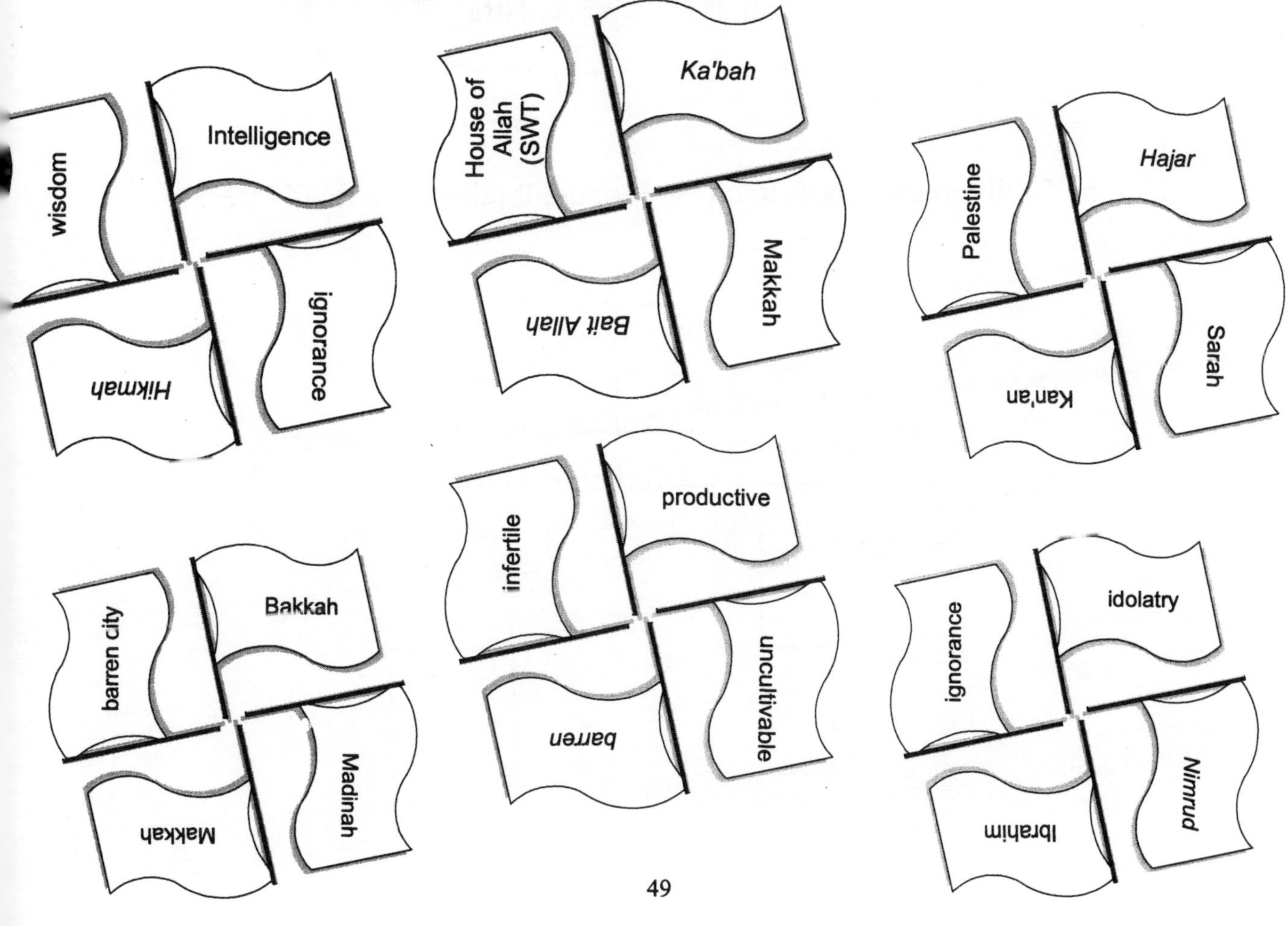

5. Family Tree

Family trees show relationships within the family. Certain symbols tell you what kind of relationship one family member has to another. A circle means that a person is a female (○); a square means that a person is male (□). A husband and wife are represented by a horizontal line (—). Children are represented by a vertical line (|). Branching lines that can be traced back to the original vertical line represent brothers and sisters (┌┴┐).

EXAMPLE: Nūr is 'Ali's wife. Nūr and Ali have two children – their son's name is Sa'ad and their daughter's name is Hira.

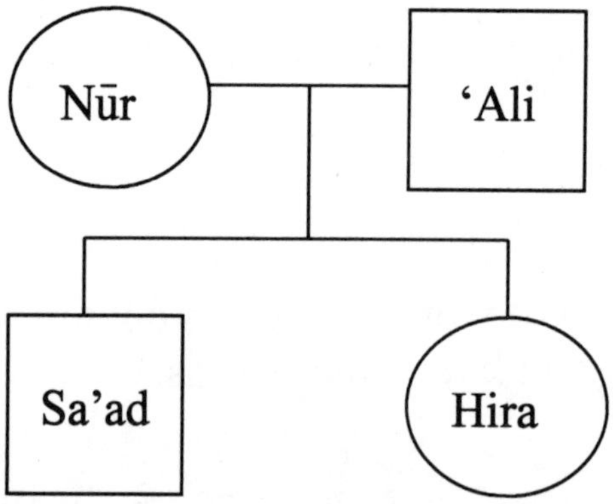

Use the family tree symbols to create Prophet Ibrāhīm's عليه السلام family tree.

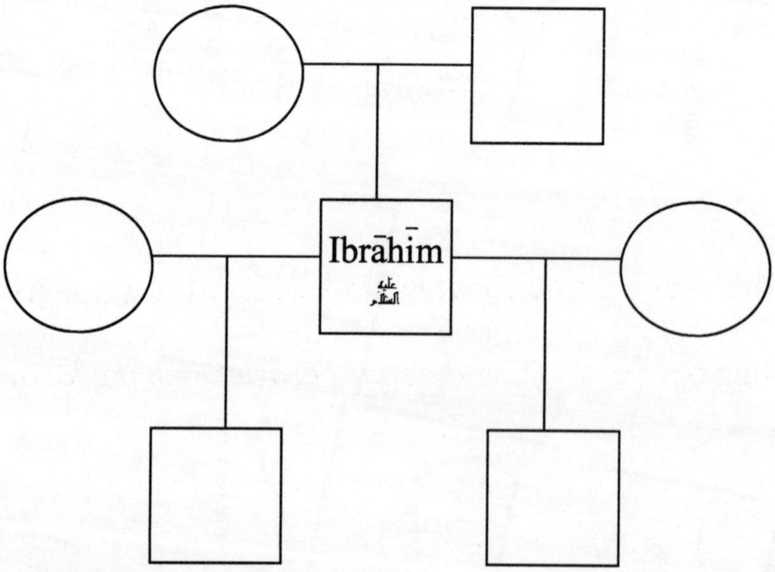

6. Qur'anic Study

The *‘āyat* below describes a debate between Prophet Ibrāhīm ﵇ and King Nimrud. After being unable to respond to Ibrāhīm's ﵇ challenge to him to raise the sun from the west, Nimrud became very angry and ordered Ibrāhīm ﵇ to be put to death rather than admit he was wrong.

أَلَمْ تَرَ إِلَى ٱلَّذِى حَآجَّ إِبْرَٰهِـۧمَ فِى رَبِّهِۦٓ أَنْ ءَاتَىٰهُ ٱللَّهُ
ٱلْمُلْكَ إِذْ قَالَ إِبْرَٰهِـۧمُ رَبِّىَ ٱلَّذِى يُحْىِۦ وَيُمِيتُ قَالَ أَنَا۠ أُحْىِۦ وَأُمِيتُ ۖ
قَالَ إِبْرَٰهِـۧمُ فَإِنَّ ٱللَّهَ يَأْتِى بِٱلشَّمْسِ مِنَ ٱلْمَشْرِقِ فَأْتِ بِهَا مِنَ ٱلْمَغْرِبِ
فَبُهِتَ ٱلَّذِى كَفَرَ ۗ وَٱللَّهُ لَا يَهْدِى ٱلْقَوْمَ ٱلظَّٰلِمِينَ ﴿٢٥٨﴾

Have you not turned your attention to the one who argued with Ibrahim about his Lord because Allah gave him power? Ibrahim said, "My Lord is He who gives life and death." He said, "I too give life and death." Ibrahim said, "But it is Allah who causes the sun to rise in the east, can you then make it rise in the west?" So the one who rejected faith was confounded. Nor does Allah give guidance to an unjust people.
(*Al-Baqarah*, 2:258)

Write your opinion about why we sometimes get angry when we are proven wrong. Is it good, according to the Qur'ān, to stick with our wrong opinions? (*Use the space provided on the following page.*)

Lesson 10

THE STORY OF THE KA'BAH

1. Sequencing

Aminah was studying for a test but all of her papers fell. Help Aminah put her notes back in proper order by numbering each page in the sequence in which it should fall. Place the number in the tab at the top of each page.

#
Banu Jarham's caravan arrived.

#
Ibrāhīm ﷺ sees a city (Makkah) in the desert.

#
Hajar could grow food.

#
Hajar and 'Ismā'īl ﷺ ran out of food and water.

#
Hajar ran up the hills of Safā and Marwah.

#
Hajar sees an angel by 'Ismā'īl ﷺ.

#
Ibrāhīm ﷺ left Hajar and 'Ismā'īl in a barren valley.

#
Hajar called the water Zamzam.

2. True/False

Mark each statement as **true** or **false**. If the statement is false, cross out what is false and fill in the appropriate information to make the statement true.

EXAMPLE: ‘Ibrahim ~~‘Ismā’īl~~ is the father of ‘Isma’il ~~‘Ibrāhīm~~.

________ Ibrāhīm took ‘Ismā’īl to Makkah to sacrifice him.

________ Allāh stopped Ibrāhīm from sacrificing his son.

________ Allāh had asked Ibrāhīm to sacrifice ‘Ismā’īl because He was upset at ‘Ismā’īl.

________ We sacrifice an animal as a part of *’Id al-‘Adhā* in remembrance of Allāh’s command to sacrifice ‘Ismā’īl.

3. Think about It!!

How did Ibrāhīm and ‘Ismā’īl react to Allāh’s command that Ibrāhīm sacrifice his son?

4. Allah's Tests

You have learned the story of how Allāh سبحانه وتعالى tested Ibrāhīm's عليه السلام faith. Sometimes bad things happen to good people, whom you may think do not deserve such things. We have to remember that these difficult times are Allāh's سبحانه وتعالى way of testing our faith in Him. In the following examples, check off which may be a test given by Allāh سبحانه وتعالى:

____ Your mother suddenly falls very sick and has to be taken to the hospital.

____ You make fun of your classmate, and your teacher gives you a detention.

____ Your car breaks down in the middle of your family vacation to Disneyworld.

____ You don't study very hard and fail a test.

____ You are a new student in school and your classmates are mean to you.

____ You ate too much candy and stayed up all night with a terrible stomach ache.

____ Your friend's house was damaged in a tornado.

4. Vocabulary

Use the following words in complete sentences:

heritage ____

____

offspring ____

____

quench ____

____

ritual ____

____

sacrifice ____

____

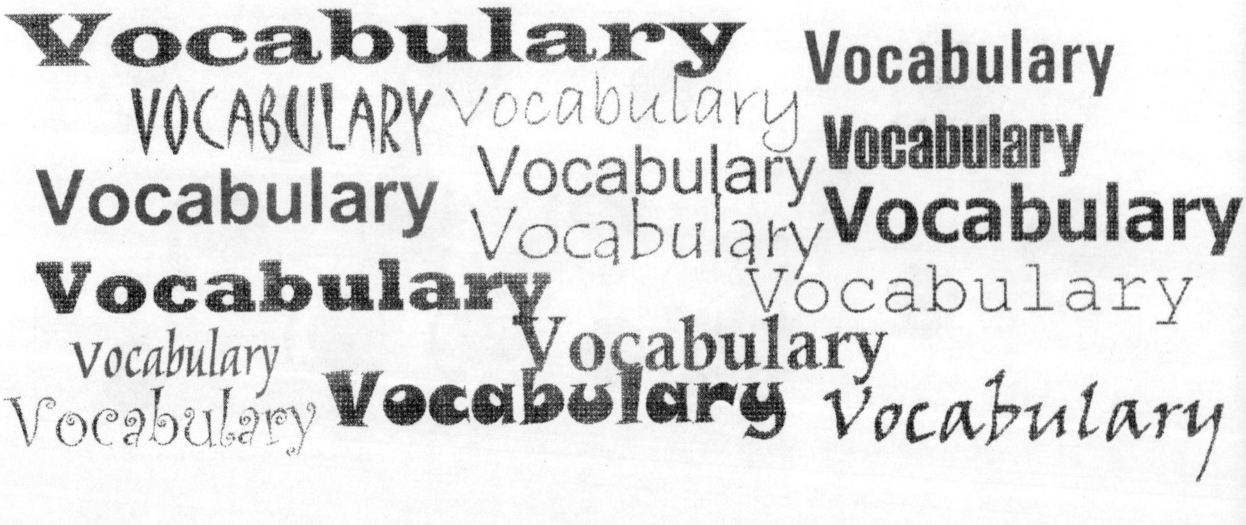

6. Qur'anic Study

The *'āyat* given below tells us that sometimes bad things happen in our lives. How does Allāh ﷻ tell us to behave during these times and why does Allāh ﷻ put us in such situations?

وَلَنَبْلُوَنَّكُم بِشَيْءٍ مِّنَ ٱلْخَوْفِ وَٱلْجُوعِ وَنَقْصٍ مِّنَ ٱلْأَمْوَٰلِ
وَٱلْأَنفُسِ وَٱلثَّمَرَٰتِ ۗ وَبَشِّرِ ٱلصَّٰبِرِينَ ﴿١٥٥﴾

Be sure that We shall test you with something from fear and hunger, some loss in property or life or your work, but give good news to those who stay patient.
(*Al-Baqarah*, 2:155)

Lesson 11

HOW TO MAKE THE ḤAJJ

1. The Fundamentals of the *Hajj*

What are the five conditions for *Ḥajj* to be *Farḍ*?

a. ______________________________

____

____

e. ______________________________

____

____

b. ______________________________

____

____

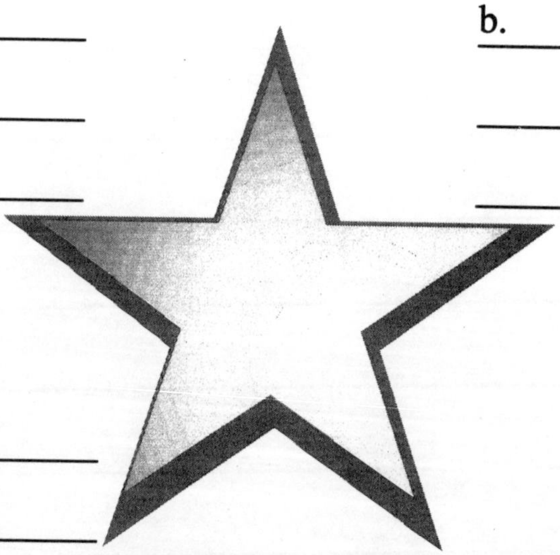

d. ______________________________

____

____

c. ______________________________

____

____

2. Words that Contain the Letter "H"

Use the following clues to figure out what the "H" words are:

The pilgrimage **H** ___ ___ ___

The person who is performing the pilgrimage. **H** ___ ___ ___

The people performing the pilgrimage. **H** ___ ___ ___ ___ ___

The Islamic month of the pilgrimage ___ **H** ___

___ ___ **H** ___ ___ ___ ___ **H**

3. Think about It!!

Why do you think it is important for the *Ḥujjāj* to put on an *'Iḥrām*?

4. Yes/No

Mark "yes" if the underlined word is used correctly in the sentence. Mark "no" if it is not, then write in the word that makes the sentence correct.

a. Asimah's *'iḥrām* is her brother, Khaleel.

YES NO

CORRECT WORD

b. The *Ḥajj* is not *Farḍ* on certain people, such as the poor, insane or children.

YES NO

CORRECT WORD

c. One of the preparations for performing the *Ḥajj* is to say the *Mīqāt*.

YES NO

CORRECT WORD

d. If you have already performed the *Ḥajj*, any other *Ḥajj* you perform is *Nafl*.

YES NO

CORRECT WORD

5. Crossword Puzzle

Fill in the boxes using the words given below. Then unscramble the letters in the heavy-lined boxes to reveal the mystery word.

WORDS: ḤAJJ, NAFL, DHU AL-ḤIJJAH, 'UMRAH, MAḤRAM, SALĀM, ḤUJJĀJ, IḤRĀM, TALBIYAH, ṢALĀH

The Mystery Word: ______________________

7. Qur'anic Study

Allāh ﷻ describes the blessings that people gain when they go on *Ḥajj*. He also mentions the difficulty many people go through to be able to perform it. Interview someone you know who has been on the *Ḥajj* and ask them about what types of difficulties they encountered and the rewards they received there.

وَأَذِّن فِى ٱلنَّاسِ بِٱلْحَجِّ يَأْتُوكَ رِجَالًا وَعَلَىٰ كُلِّ ضَامِرٍ
يَأْتِينَ مِن كُلِّ فَجٍّ عَمِيقٍ ﴿٢٧﴾

And proclaim the Ḥajj to the people; they will come to you on foot and on every kind of camel, tired on account of journeys through difficult and far highways.
(*Al-Ḥajj*, 22:27)

Lesson 12

PERFORMING THE ḤAJJ: THE 'UMRAH

1. Sequencing

Put the following statements regarding *'Umrah* in the correct sequential order (place sequencing number in box provided):

- [ ] The *Ḥajj* makes a special *Du'ā* at the *Multazam.*
- [ ] The *Ḥajj* performs *Halq* or *Taqsīr.*
- [ ] The *Ḥajj* drinks water from the *Zamzam* well standing and facing the *Ka'bah.*
- [ ] The *Ḥajj* puts on his *Iḥrām*
- [ ] The *Ḥajj* performs *Tawāf.*
- [ ] The *Ḥajj* prays two *Raka'āt* at the *Maqām 'Ibrāhīm* or any other place at the *Ḥaram.*
- [ ] The *Ḥajj* removes his *Iḥrām.*
- [ ] The *Ḥajj* performs the *Sā'ī.*

2. Mystery Word

Clues are given to help you figure out the mystery word. Fill in the blanks with the correct spelling.

CLUE: I am very refreshing.

WORD: **Z** __ __ __ __ __

CLUE: A prophet left something of his behind here.

WORD: **M** __ __ __ __ ‘__ __ __ __ __ __ __

CLUE: A woman cannot do this.

WORD: **H** __ __ __

3. Think about It!!

Why do you think there is a strict sequential order while performing *‘Umrah*?

____

____

____

____

____

____

4. Vocabulary - *Synonym Search*

A synonym is a word that has approximately the same meaning as another word. For example, "happy" and "glad" are synonyms. Use a dictionary or thesaurus to find synonyms for the following words. Remember, a synonym is <u>one word</u>, not many words giving a definition.

a. *Sā'ī* ____________________

b. reward ____________________

c. remove ____________________

d. special ____________________

e. preserve ____________________

f. brisk ____________________

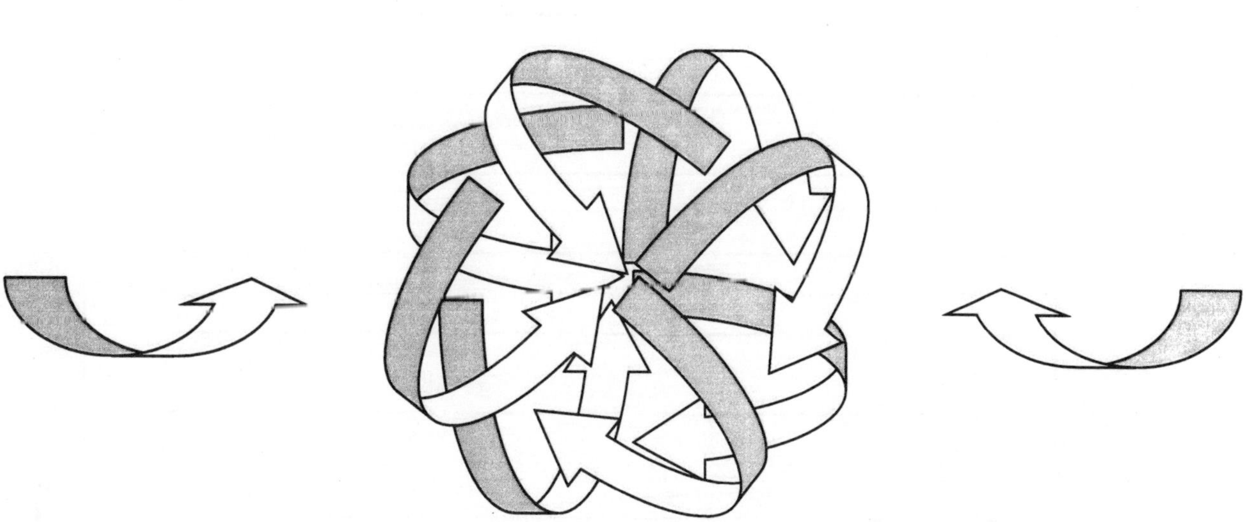

5. Qur'anic Study

Describe what *hujjāj* have to do when visiting the two hills mentioned in the *'āyah* given below and where this ritual originated.

﴿ إِنَّ ٱلصَّفَا وَٱلْمَرْوَةَ مِن شَعَآئِرِ ٱللَّهِ ۖ

Behold! Ṣafā and Marwah are among the symbols of Allāh.
(*Al-Baqarah*, 2:158)

Lesson 13

PERFORMING THE ḤAJJ: THE COMPLETION

1. Why Is This Important?

Indicate what is the importance of each of the following events during *Ḥajj:*

Sacrifice an animal

____

____

____

____

Stay at Muzdalifah

____

____

____

____

Throw stones at the *Jamarāt*

____

____

____

____

Stay at the valley of 'Arafāt

____

____

____

____

Trip to Makkah to visit the *Ḥaram*

____

____

____

____

2. Fill in the Blanks

The *Ḥujjāj* make *Ḥajj* between the ____th and the ____th of ____________________.

3. Think about It!!

What did Rasūlullāh ﷺ mean when he said that one who performs *Ḥajj* will "revert to (the purity of) the day of his/her birth"? (*Al-Bukhari, 'Ahmad, An-Nisa'i)*

____

____

____

____

____

4. Learning on Your Own - *'Id Dates*

Find an Islamic calendar and a Gregorian calendar. Since you know the dates of *Ḥajj* on the Islamic calendar, use that information to figure out what the dates for *Ḥajj* are for <u>this year</u> on the Gregorian calendar (*see Appendix A*).

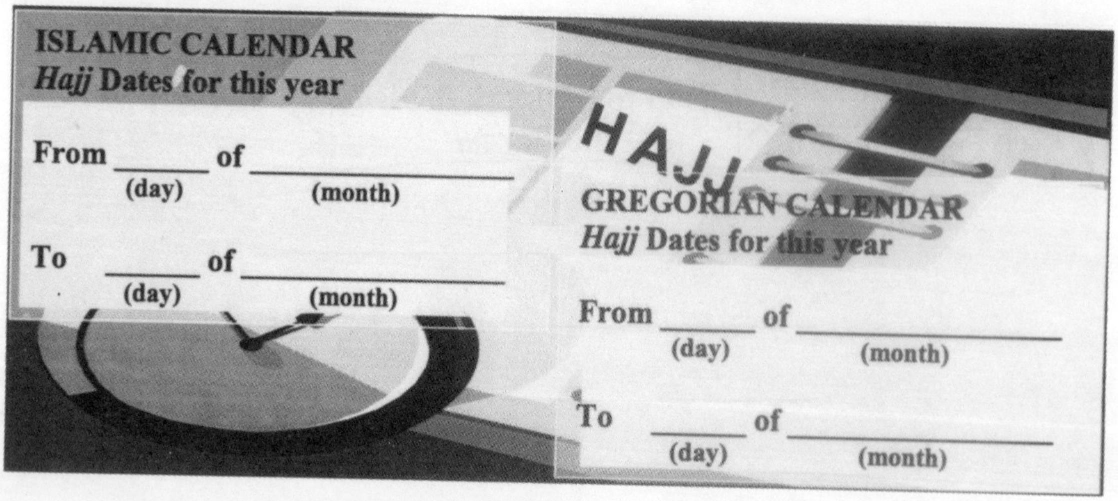

5. Vocabulary

Use the clues given to unscramble the letters and form words (*the words are given below)*:
WORDS: ***muzdalifah, jamrah, khutbah al-wada, jamarat, iḥram, tawaf az-ziyarah***

M T R A A J A

We collect pebbles for them.

__ __ __ __ __ __ __

H J A R A M

Singular for the above answer.

__ __ __ __ __ __

"Circumambulation of the visit."

R A Z A Ṭ F H A W Z Y A I

__ __ __ __ __ __ __ __ __ __ __ __ __

M I Ḥ R A

White cloth.

__ __ __ __ __

Important sermon in history.

A K W L B A U H D A T A H

__ __ __ __ __ __ __ __ __ __ __ __ __

Z A L I M F U D H A

__ __ __ __ __ __ __ __ __ __

Valley where the *Ḥujjāj* stay.

6. Qur'anic Study

Reading the following *'ayat*, what is the Holy Place one must visit following the departure from 'Arafat?

لَيۡسَ عَلَيۡكُمۡ جُنَاحٌ

أَن تَبۡتَغُواْ فَضۡلٗا مِّن رَّبِّكُمۡۚ فَإِذَآ أَفَضۡتُم مِّنۡ عَرَفَٰتٖ فَٱذۡكُرُواْ

ٱللَّهَ عِندَ ٱلۡمَشۡعَرِ ٱلۡحَرَامِۖ وَٱذۡكُرُوهُ كَمَا هَدَىٰكُمۡ وَإِن كُنتُم مِّن قَبۡلِهِۦ

لَمِنَ ٱلضَّآلِّينَ ﴿١٩٨﴾

Then when you come down from 'Arafat make remembrance of Allah at the Holy Place and chant His praises as He has directed you even though, before this, you went astray.
(*Al-Baqarah*, 2:198)

Lesson 14

THE ZIYĀRAH OF MADĪNAH

1. Think about It!!

Why is Madīnah such an important city in Islamic history?

____

____

____

____

____

2. Matching

Draw a line from the *masjid* to the place where it is located.

a. *Masjid al-'Aqsa'*

c. *al-Musjid al-Ḥaram*

b. *Masjid an-Nabī*

d. *al-Masjid Qubā*

Makkah

Outside of Madīnah

Ma īnah

Jerusalem

3. Why Is This Important?

What important event in Islamic history does the *Masjid al-Qiblatain* commemorate?

____

____

____

____

____

____

____

____

4. Important People in Islamic History

Put a check mark next to the names of the people who are buried in Madīnah. Next to the checked persons' names, indicate how they were related to Rasūlullāh ﷺ. (Mercy to Mankind, *lessons 21 & 22)*

- Ḥamzah رضي الله عنه ______________________________
- 'Uthmān رضي الله عنه ______________________________
- 'Alī رضي الله عنه ______________________________
- Khadīja رضي الله عنها ______________________________
- 'Abū Bakr رضي الله عنه ______________________________
- 'Ā'ishah رضي الله عنها ______________________________
- 'Umar رضي الله عنه ______________________________

5. Vocabulary

Use the following words in your own sentences:

Ziyārāt(h) ______________________________

____

Thawāb ______________________________

____

pious ______________________________

____

commemorates ______________________________

____

6. Qur'anic Study

Using a Qur'ānic index, look up verses that talk about foods and those that are *ḥarām* or *ḥalāl*.

Lesson 15

JIHĀD I: STRUGGLE WITH WEALTH AND WITH PERSONS

1. Adjective Acronyms

An **adjective** is a word that describes a noun (examples: green, sandy, lovely). **Acronyms** are words that are created by combining the first letters of a series of words. Come up with adjectives describing the words below, being sure to use each letter of the word as the first letter of the adjectives.

EXAMPLE:

A lmighty

L oving

L ast

A ll knowing

H oly

J ____________________

I ____________________

H ____________________

Ā ____________________

D ____________________

M ____________________

Ā ____________________

L ____________________

2. Vocabulary

Match the term with its definition.

Ṣadaqah	An obligatory payment to the poor
Hadayah	A voluntary charity in the name of Allāh سبحانه وتعالى
Zakāh	Holy war
Jihād	Holy pilgrimage
Hajj	Gifts
	Struggle in the way of Allāh سبحانه وتعالى

3. Think about It!!

How are these words alike? Think beyond the obvious similarities. What hidden relationships might the words have?

EXAMPLE: fish/soap
- both are associated with water
- both are able to float

a. *Jihād/ Ṣawm*
- ______________________________
- ______________________________

b. mosque/house
- ______________________________
- ______________________________

c. Qur'ān/encyclopedia
- ______________________________
- ______________________________

4. Finish the Thought...

Many non-Muslims misunderstand *jihād* because...

____

____

____

____

____

____

5. Qur'anic Study

What are some ways that Muslims can make *jihād*?

وَٱلَّذِينَ جَـٰهَدُوا۟ فِينَا لَنَهْدِيَنَّهُمْ سُبُلَنَا

Those who make jihād for Our cause, We will certainly guide them on Our Path."
(*Al-'Ankabūt*, 29:69)

Lesson 16

JIHĀD II: FIGHTING IN THE WAY OF ALLĀH سبحانه وتعالى

1. Questions to Think About

a. Under what circumstances are Muslims allowed to wage war?

In case of defends your self

b. If a Muslim is victorious in *Jihād*, how must he conduct himself?

They have to be humble because the victory is to Allah.

2. What Do I Do?

Muneebah is at school. She looks at her watch and sees that there is very little time left to pray *Ẓuhr*, however she is in the middle of science class. What should she do?

~~She should say if that she~~

She should asked the teacher to pray

3. Which Does Not Belong?

Read each group of words/phrases. Indicate which word/phrase does not belong with the group, then explain why.

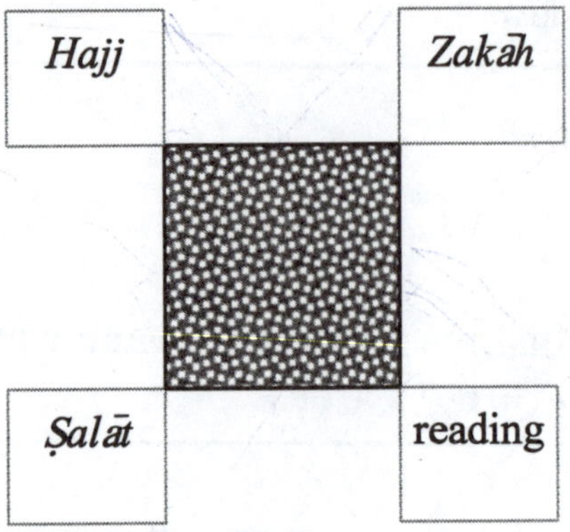

Why does the one you indicated not belong?

read, because those three are pillar of Islam

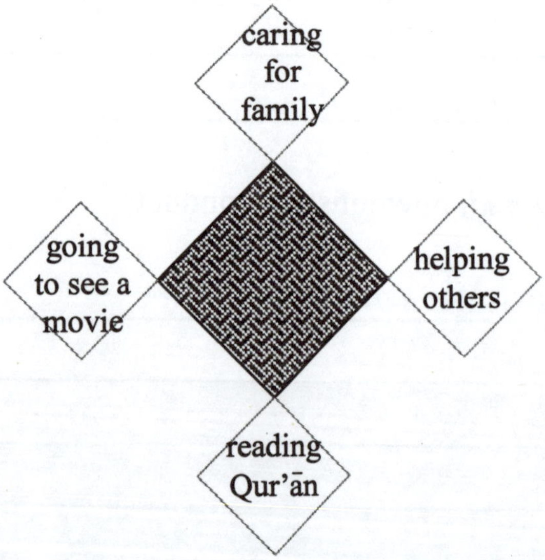

Why does the one you indicated not belong?

going to see Movie, because those thre are helping other and your self

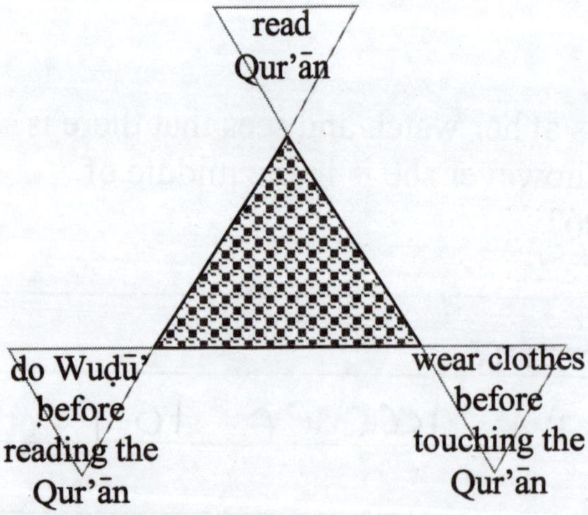

Why does the one you indicated not belong?

read, because those two are how to do before th read Quran

4. Vocabulary

Use the following words to write a paragraph about *Jihād*. Circle the vocabulary words.

defend	oppressed	righteous
rights	law	responsibility

5. Qur'anic Study

Review the *'āyat* given below. What good reasons do you think are sometimes needed to fight wars? What are some bad reasons?

وَمَا لَكُمْ لَا تُقَـٰتِلُونَ فِى

سَبِيلِ ٱللَّهِ وَٱلْمُسْتَضْعَفِينَ مِنَ ٱلرِّجَالِ وَٱلنِّسَآءِ وَٱلْوِلْدَٰنِ ٱلَّذِينَ يَقُولُونَ

رَبَّنَآ أَخْرِجْنَا مِنْ هَـٰذِهِ ٱلْقَرْيَةِ ٱلظَّالِمِ أَهْلُهَا وَٱجْعَل لَّنَا مِن لَّدُنكَ وَلِيًّا

وَٱجْعَل لَّنَا مِن لَّدُنكَ وَلِيًّا وَٱجْعَل لَّنَا مِن لَّدُنكَ

نَصِيرًا ﴿٧٥﴾

And why should you not fight in the cause of Allah and of those who, being weak, are ill-treated (and oppressed)?- Men, women, and children, whose cry is: "Our Lord! Rescue us from this town, whose people are oppressors; and raise for us from You one who will protect; and raise for us from You one who will help!" (*An-Nisā'*, 4:75)

Lesson 17

JIHĀD III: THE STRUGGLE WITHIN THE SELF

1. Think about It!!

Give three examples of personal *Jihād* that you encounter in your daily life:

2. Question to Think About

Why is *Jihād-an-Nafs* the most important according to Rasūlullāh ﷺ?

3. Word Changers

You will make a list of words by changing letters.

EXAMPLE: <u>P</u> <u>O</u> <u>S</u> <u>T</u>   office

            <u>L</u> <u>O</u> <u>S</u> <u>T</u>   and found

Not first, but   <u>L</u> <u>A</u> <u>S</u> <u>T</u>

A   <u>L</u> <u>I</u> <u>S</u> <u>T</u>   of names

Jihād an- **N** __ __ __

Arabic word meaning "voluntary"   __ __ __ __

Prophet Nūh ﷺ built a big ship to escape the   __ __ __ __ __

Unbelievers will be burned in the Fire's   __ __ __ __ __

Allāh ﷻ has 99   __ __ __ __ __

Muslims have to lead a **P** __ __ __ life.

Arabic word meaning "light"   __ __ __

Name of a prophet   __ __ __ عليه السلام

Battle of   __ __ __ __

Arabic word meaning "One"   __ __ __ __

4. True/False

Fill in the blank spaces in the table below using "true" or "false".

	It is a place	It is not *Farḍ*	It is in the Qur'ān	We are responsible for it
Jannah				
Jihād				
Jahannam				
Ṣadaqah				
Da'wah				

5. Graphic Organizer

Graphic organizers are used to organize and order ideas so that relationships between information can be seen. Use the graphic organizer below to fill in the three kinds of *Jihād*.

JIH D

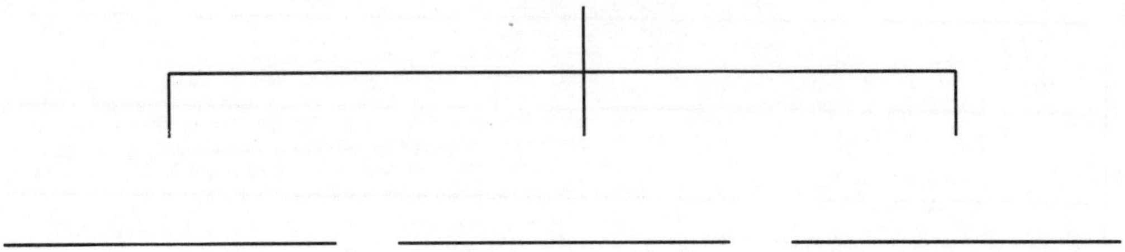

6. Qur'anic Study

In the following *'āyah* Allāh ﷻ speaks of the need for us to be fair sometimes when it is hard to. Why do you think this *Jihād* within ourselves is more difficult?

يَـٰٓأَيُّهَا ٱلَّذِينَ ءَامَنُوا۟ كُونُوا۟ قَوَّٰمِينَ لِلَّهِ شُهَدَآءَ بِٱلْقِسْطِ ۖ وَلَا يَجْرِمَنَّكُمْ
شَنَـَٔانُ قَوْمٍ عَلَىٰٓ أَلَّا تَعْدِلُوا۟ ۚ ٱعْدِلُوا۟ هُوَ أَقْرَبُ لِلتَّقْوَىٰ ۖ وَٱتَّقُوا۟ ٱللَّهَ ۚ إِنَّ ٱللَّهَ
خَبِيرٌۢ بِمَا تَعْمَلُونَ ﴿٨﴾

O ye who believe! stand out firmly for Allāh, as witnesses to fair dealing, and let not the hatred of others to you make you swerve to wrong and depart from justice. Be just: that is next to Piety: and fear Allāh. For Allāh is well-acquainted with all that ye do.
(*Al-Mā'ida*, 5:8)

Lesson 18

ISLAMIC *SHARĪ'AH*

1. What Was the Question?

Zainab fell asleep in class. The teacher asked some questions, but Zainab only woke up when someone gave an answer. Help her figure out what the questions are.

a. The Arabic language, *Fiqh*, Qur'ān and *Hadīth* are some examples.

____

____

b. *Ḥalāl*, *Ḥarām*, and *Mubāh*.

____

____

c. Because the Qur'ān is in Arabic.

____

____

d. Because it is the complete way of life.

____

____

2. Odd Word Out

Circle the word that does not go with the group of words describing the main word:

HADĪTH	Rasūlullāh ﷺ	*Sunnah*	Qur'ān	Part of *Sharī'ah*
SHARĪ'AH	*Hadīth*	*Sunnah*	Qur'ān	*'Ulamā'*
'ULAMĀ'	knowledgeable	old	pious	teachers
SĪRAH	stories	prophet	*surah*	biography

3. Learning on Your Own - *Islamic Scholars*

The textbook lists several subjects of study that a future *Faqīh* must study and master. Visit your school library, an Islamic bookstore, or your home library and list various other subjects that a *Faqīh* must know about. Write a subject on each of the title pages for the following books:

4. Vocabulary

Match the term with its definition.

Faqīh	The stories of the Prophet عليه السلام
Mubāh	The Science of *<u>Sh</u>arī'ah*
'Ulamā	To understand
Fiqh	Forbidden
Sīrah	Interpretation
Faqaha	Permissible
Tafsīr	Religious scholars
	One who masters *fiqh*

5. Qur'anic Study

What does the following *'āyat* say about whom we should obey? What do we have to obey those in charge of us after Allāh ﷻ and His Prophet ﷺ? What should we do if we fail to find the answer from our leaders and scholars?

يَٰٓأَيُّهَا ٱلَّذِينَ ءَامَنُوٓاْ أَطِيعُواْ ٱللَّهَ وَأَطِيعُواْ ٱلرَّسُولَ وَأُوْلِي ٱلۡأَمۡرِ
مِنكُمۡۖ فَإِن تَنَٰزَعۡتُمۡ فِي شَيۡءٖ فَرُدُّوهُ إِلَى ٱللَّهِ وَٱلرَّسُولِ إِن كُنتُمۡ
تُؤۡمِنُونَ بِٱللَّهِ وَٱلۡيَوۡمِ ٱلۡأٓخِرِۚ ذَٰلِكَ خَيۡرٞ وَأَحۡسَنُ تَأۡوِيلًا ٥٩

O ye who believe! obey Allāh, and obey the Messenger, and those charged with authority among you. If ye differ in anything among yourselves, refer it to Allāh and His Messenger, if ye do believe in Allāh and the Last Day: that is best, and most suitable for final determination.

(*An-Nisā'*, 4:59)

Lesson 19

ḤALĀL AND ḤARĀM: EARNING

1. *Halal* or *Haram*

Indicate in the following examples whether they are *Ḥalāl* (H) or *Ḥarām* (N) ways of earning money.

Accepting bribery to cover up someone's mistake at work

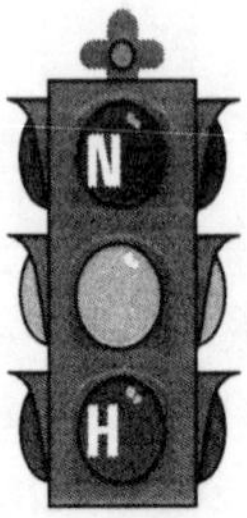

Winning the lottery

Inheriting your uncle's house

Selling crops from your land

Working overtime

Loaning someone money and having it paid back with interest

Working as a bartender

2. Think about It!!

Give your own example of a *Ḥarām* way of earning and describe why it is displeasing to Allāh (SWT).

____

____

____

____

Give your own example of a *Ḥalāl* way of earning and describe why it is pleasing to Allāh ﷾.

____

____

____

____

3. Word Changers

You will make a list of words by changing letters.

EXAMPLE:	P	O	S	T	office
	L	O	S	T	and found
Not first, but	L	A	S	T	
A	L	I	S	T	of names

We must **E** ___ ___ ___ our money by *Ḥalāl* means

Allāh ﷻ ___ ___ ___ ___ (s) us of *Jahannum.*

Not hot, not cold, but ___ ___ ___ ___

Allāh ﷻ will not let anyone ___ ___ ___ ___ you, if you follow the Right Path

Allāh ﷻ promises us great ___ ___ ___ ___ ___ ___ for doing good deeds

Everything we have is a **G** ___ ___ ___ from Allāh ﷻ

By praying, we ___ ___ ___ ___ our spirits

Salma made a shopping ___ ___ ___ ___

Muhammad ﷺ is Allāh's ﷻ ___ ___ ___ ___ prophet

3. Antonyms

An **antonym** is a word that means the opposite of a given word. For example, "good" is an antonym of "bad". Write down the antonyms for the following words:

Ḥalāl ____________________

secure ____________________

rich ____________________

Barakah ____________________

profits ____________________

just ____________________

5. Qur'anic Study

Reading this *'āyat*, what can we understand about the importance of *Jumu'a Ṣalāt*? Is it permitted to work after we finish our prayer?

يَٰٓأَيُّهَا ٱلَّذِينَ ءَامَنُوٓاْ إِذَا نُودِيَ لِلصَّلَوٰةِ مِن يَوۡمِ ٱلۡجُمُعَةِ فَٱسۡعَوۡاْ إِلَىٰ
ذِكۡرِ ٱللَّهِ وَذَرُواْ ٱلۡبَيۡعَۚ ذَٰلِكُمۡ خَيۡرٞ لَّكُمۡ إِن كُنتُمۡ تَعۡلَمُونَ ٩

O ye who believe! When the call is proclaimed to prayer on Friday (the Day of Assembly), hasten earnestly to the Remembrance of Allah, and leave off business (and traffic): that is best for you if ye but knew! (*Al-Jumu'a*, 62:9)

Lesson 20

ḤALĀL AND ḤARĀM: FOOD AND DRINKS

1. Think about It!!

There are certain manners that Muslims follow when eating. List two of them and describe why they are important.

____

____

____

____

2. Vocabulary

Use the following words in complete sentences:

Ḥalāl ____

____

Ḥarām ____

____

Dhabīhah ____

____

Mashrik ____

____

Barakah ____

____

Najās ____

____

3. What Do I Do?

Fatimah's class is having a picnic. The school cafeteria makes ham and cheese sandwiches for the students to eat. What should Fatimah do?

____

____

____

____

____

4. Research

Check the ingredients of food products you have in your home. Have you found anything that might be *Ḥarām* that your parents might have accidentally bought?

____

____

____

____

6. Qur'anic Study

وَكُلُوا۟ مِمَّا رَزَقَكُمُ ٱللَّهُ حَلَـٰلًا طَيِّبًا ۚ وَٱتَّقُوا۟ ٱللَّهَ ٱلَّذِىٓ أَنتُم بِهِۦ مُؤْمِنُونَ ﴿٨٨﴾

Eat of that which Allāh has given you as good, lawful food and keep your duty to Allāh in whom you believe. (Al-Mā'idah, 5:88)

In each scroll below, list the types of foods that are *Ḥalāl* and can be eaten, and *Ḥarām* and cannot be eaten.

☑ *Ḥalāl* ☑	☒ *Ḥarām* ☒
______________________	______________________
______________________	______________________
______________________	______________________
______________________	______________________
______________________	______________________
______________________	______________________
______________________	______________________
______________________	______________________
______________________	______________________
______________________	______________________
______________________	______________________

Appendix A

OUR ISLAMIC CALENDAR

People have always invented a way to keep track of the time of year. Since very ancient days humans have used calendars. Most calendars are based on the movement of objects in space, such as the sun, moon and stars.

The Gregorian Calendar

The calendar that is used world-wide today is based on one that was developed by the ancient Romans and later transferred to the Christians. This is called the Gregorian calendar, named after Pope Gregory XIII, the leader of the Roman Catholic Church from 1565 to 1585. This calendar is based on the movement of the sun and lasts 365 days. It consists of the following months:

January	**July**
February	**August**
March	**September**
April	**October**
May	**November**
June	**December**

The Islamic Calendar

The Islamic calendar is different from the Gregorian calendar because it is based on the movements of the moon. Every time the new moon appears in the sky a new Islamic month begins. Like the Gregorian calendar, the Islamic calendar has twelve months. The Islamic year lasts about 354 days and it slowly moves through the seasons, so that Ramaḍan, for example, will be in the winter one year and many years later it will fall in the summer! The months of the Islamic calendar are as follows:

Muḥarram	**Rajab**
Ṣafar	**Sha'bān**
Rabī' al-Awwal	**Ramaḍān**
Rabī' al-Thāni	**Shawwāl**
Jumādā al-'Ūlā	**Dhu al-Qa'dah**
Jumādā al-'Ākhirah	**Dhu al-Ḥijjah**

Another difference between the two calendars is that the Gregorian calendar starts from the supposed birth of Jesus ('Isa ﵇). The Islamic calendar starts from the *Hijrah* of the Prophet Muhammad ﷺ from Makkah to Madinah.